DR. FIRESIGN'S FOLLIES

Radio, Comedy, Mystery, History

by David Ossman

ALSO BY DAVID OSSMAN

NOVEL
The Ronald Reagan Murder Case

POETRY
Radio Poems (Turkey Press, Isla Vista): The Moonsign Book,
The Day-Book of the City, The Rainbow Café, Hopi Set
Set in a Landscape
The Crescent Journals
Pablo Neruda — The Early Poems
(with Carlos Hagen)

INTERVIEWS
The Sullen Art

AUDIO PLAYS
The Wonderful Wizard of Oz
Gulliver's Travels
Empire of the Air
Raymond Chandler's "Goldfish"
The Red Badge of Courage

THEATRE
Seven Keys to Baldpate (G. M. Cohan)
Through the Looking Glass (Lewis Carroll)
The Little Wizard Stories (with Judith Walcutt)
Love Is a Place: an E. E. Cummings Cabaret
The Winter Visit (with Martha Furey)
Electrician & Dwarf: A Firesign Theatre Double-Bill

CD AUDIO
The George Tirebiter Collection
New and Found Poems in Performance
How Time Flys

ANTHOLOGIES (Editor)
The Firesign Theatre's Big Book of Plays
The Firesign Theatre's Big Mystery Joke Book

DR. FIRESIGN'S FOLLIES: RADIO, COMEDY, MYSTERY, HISTORY
STARRING FORMER SURREALIST CELEBRITY GEORGE L. TIREBITER
© 2008 DAVID OSSMAN

All rights reserved.

Some parts of this collection were first published in a different form in "The Firesign Theatre's Big Book of Plays," *Crawdaddy Magazine*, various CD booklets from Original Master Recordings, the *Santa Barbara News & Review*, the *Santa Barbara News-Press*, publications of the Midwest Radio Theatre Workshop and National Audio Theatre Festivals, The Mark Time and Ogle Awards and other sources. The radio scripts were first presented on the air (KPFK, XM Satellite Radio) or on stage (Whidbey Island Center for the Arts). Live-on-stage performances of these and other radio shows are available in "The George Tirebiter Collection," a 5-CD set published by Otherworld Media. My thanks to all of these friendly publishers and programmers and always to my partners in the Firesign Theatre for their ever-antic contributions to The Work.

Photographs and other illustrations from The Ossman Archive.

Campoon '76 photo coverage mostly by Patricia Pence. Campoon graphics by Joe Beets, Gizmo Brothers and other anonymous artists. All rights reversed. Mark Time logo by William Stout. Mark Time Awards logo designed by Chris Jones. How Time Flys illustration by Joe Garnett.

George Tirebiter, himself, has his own website at www.georgetirebiter.com.

For complete information about The Firesign Theatre, please consult www.firesigntheatre.com.

For publication or performance rights to Ossman and Firesign scripts, write oworld@whidbey.com.

For a complete history of the Mark Time and Ogle Awards go to www.greatnorthernaudio.com/MarkTime/MarkTime.html.

No part of this book may be reproduced in any form or by any means, electronic, mechanical, digital, photocopying or recording, except for the inclusion in a review, without permission in writing from the the publisher.

Published in the USA by:

BearManor Media
PO Box 71426
Albany, GA 31708
www.BearManorMedia.com

LIBRARY OF CONGRESS CATALOGING-IN-PUBLICATION DATA:

Ossman, David.
  [Selections]
  Dr. Firesign's follies : radio, comedy, mystery, history / by David Ossman.
     p. cm.
  Includes bibliographical references and index.
  ISBN 978-1-62933-347-2
  I. Title.

PS3615.S63A6 2008
813'.6--dc22

2008019512

Printed in the United States
Design and Layout by Valerie Thompson

The Pitch

Welcome to the Funway, Bozos! I've designed five thrilling entertainment packages for your reading pleasure. First, enter the Firesign Theatre Time Machine with a many-mirrored introduction to the best-known ten of the Firesign's more than twenty comedy CDs, and to some of the events and ideas that inspired them, collected from liner notes, out-of-print essays and my journals, clip files and other entertaining sources.

Then, after a 24/7 Movie Matinee with Ben Bland, there's no waiting in line for a double-dose of my personal radio hero, George Tirebiter! First, rock out with George's scandal-filled cross-country run for Surrealist Vice President of the U. S. Then, wander a gallery of little-known contributors to American history — the fabled Poon Family — all of them Surrealist 'Resident George Papoon's colorful ancestors (Tirebiter is a distant relation too!).

After that, take a break with "Off the Wall," where the past, present and future are quizzically chronicled in easy-to-digest doses of journalistic jive. They're quickly followed by dueling Editorial Comments from Brother Bill Barnstormer and Beat St. Jack.

Finally, get with the programs! I'll close this book with a "behind the mic" exhibition of the Arts and Crafts of Radio Theatre. With my Radio Primer and a few favorite scripts we can revisit perilous Planet X with Commander Mark Time; wander "over the edge" with Poor Peggy; motor up the Coast Highway with crime cabby Maxwell Morgan; and set Mr. Tirebiter off on his most surreal and perplexing mystery yet.
DAVID OSSMAN
WHIDBEY ISLAND 2007

"The Pitch"

Dr. Firesign's Follies

CONTENTS

INTRODUCTION
TIREBITER LIVES BY PHIL PROCTOR . . . 4

PART ONE:
THE FIRESIGN THEATRE
TIME TRAVELING FROM OZ TO MARS . . . 9
"I'M BEN BLAND" — A COMMERCIAL INTERLUDE . . . 65

PART TWO:
TIREBITER FOR VEEP!
THE INSIDE SAGA OF CAMPOON '76 . . . 75

PART THREE:
THE ROOTS OF POON
6 TALES FROM THE UNTOLD HISTORY OF THE USA . . . 107

PART FOUR:
OFF THE WALL!
ALTERNATIVE WIT AND WISDOM . . . 139
BROTHER BILL VS. BEAT ST. JACK — EDITORIAL COUNTERPOINT . . . 167

PART FIVE:
FUN WITH RADIO THEATRE
COMEDY, MYSTERY, SCI-FI, SCRIPTS AND TIPS . . . 175
"WHO'S PEGGY?," "MAX MORGAN," "MARK TIME"
"THE GEORGE TIREBITER MYSTERY"

Tirebiter Lives!

BY PHIL PROCTOR

Dear friends, I'm sure you've all heard the old newspaper editor's pep talk to the cub reporter: "Son, when a dog bites a man, that's not a story, but when a man bites a dog — that's a headline!"

Well, decades ago, when the rookie members of the newly-formed Firesign Theatre first sat around an old wooden table in a smoke-filled room at one of our Southern Californian cribs to rough out the story and characters for an album based on our 1969 stage presentation, called "A Life in the Day" or "The TV Set" depending on which show you saw, all about channel-surfing before it was invented — we mutually agreed on the name "Peorge Tirebiter" for our young protagonist, to be played, it turned out, by Mr. David Ossman, or "Dave Casman," as credited by the TV announcer for "The Howl of the Wolf" late-night movie presentation of the film "High School Madness!"

Now, you see, this character's name was based on a legendary . . . dog.

That's what I said. A cute, scruffy mutt known for manically chasing cars near USC on University Avenue, who became a mascot of sorts in the '40s and '50s when he began, quite on his own, attending football games and often rushing onto the field, once impulsively biting the UCLA mascot Joe Bruin on the nose — perhaps, as it's been suggested in Steve Harvey's *L.A. Times'* "Only in L.A." column, "in retaliation for the time he was dog-napped and had 'UCLA' shaved into his fur."

Well, now he's been immortalized in bronze right next to Tommy Trojan on the USC campus, wearing a sweater with "USC" on it (knitted to cover his shameful shaving), next to a stack of bronzed

"What a Wonderful Supper!"
(Phil Proctor as Prince Edmund)
Photo by Lee Greathouse

tires with a football on top and an engraved marble slab telling his story.

Oh, did I mention? His name is "George Tirebiter."

Somehow, over the evolution of that record, "George LEROY Tirebiter" was born, incarnated as the older actor who played "Peorge" in our classic, totally bogus 1950s anti-communist film and who was later blacklisted for his pacifist views.

The album, ultimately titled "Don't Crush that Dwarf, Hand Me the Pliers" (based on a WWI anti-Hun song that . . . oh, don't get me started!), was recently inducted into the U.S. Library of Congress Historical Recordings Archives at a ceremony in Washington AC/DC, where we got to actually perform an excerpt from the recording.

Some of the other 50 inductees include Fanny Brice, Fred Allen, Bob Hope, Fats Domino, Jerry Lee Lewis, Paul (Tubby the Tuba) Tripp, Count Basie, Arturo Toscanini, Paul Robeson, Nat "King" Cole, Stevie Wonder, B.B. King, Frank Zappa, Jimi Hendrix, Martha Reeves of Martha and the Vandellas, Archibald MacLeish's "Fall of the City," the 1938 Joe Louis-Max Schmeling fight — and the old foghorn at Kewaunee, Wisconsin. What great company! But I digress . . .

A few years after "Dwarf" hit the stores and became a monster hit for us, when the group ran the masked candidate George Papoon for President under the banner of the National Surrealist Martian Space Party, GLT signed on as his vice-presidential running mate; and that's where our friend David Ossman seems to have lost it — or found it, as the case may be.

From that day on, and through many incarnations, David embraced, and at times, it appears, assumed, the character of this entirely fictitious creation of our fevered brains, to the point where "he" has taken on a life of "his" own.

David Ossman/Dave Casman/Peorge/George Leroy Tirebiter; Surrealist Party vice-presidential candidate; legendary actor/writer/producer from radio's Golden Age; author of the "true stories" of his fabled adventures in Hollywood's storied past . . . Hey! Who exactly AM he, anyway?

It brings to mind (or what's left of it) the classic Firesign query posed so many years ago in "Dwarf" — "What is reality?'

Well, that's a question better left unanswered; but here's my headline for you to ponder while you enter George's multi-layered, sometimes downright hallucinogenic world:

"Dog BECOMES Man!"

WOOF! PHIL PROCTOR,
BEVERLY HELL, 06/06/06

PART ONE

DO, Lit & Drama Director, KPFK, 1963

The Firesign Theatre

TIME TRAVELING FROM OZ TO MARS

1. WHERE THE SOUND COMES FROM

An essay prepared for the School of Sound seminars in London, trying to bring a primarily European audience into the experience of American radio and so into the early work of The Firesign Theatre. (2005)

Sound — the "thingness" of Sound — began for me with the Sound of the Radio: distant voices from Broadway theatre stages; Hollywood hotel dance bands with their un-hip announcers; Bob Hope getting laugh after laugh in front of a huge Army audience. And all of it coming to you live!

Earlier, although I heard it first much later, the Amazing Lindberg Broadcast, where half-a-dozen intrepid newsmen, including the Metropolitan Opera's silken-toned Milton Cross and the archetypal radio voice of authority, Graham McNamee, achieved the first multi-point live news coverage event — in 1927!

The War of the Worlds — not the one in '38 — I didn't hear that until the '50s — but WWII at Pearl Harbor in 1941, along with *Latitude Zero* — an adventure serial that must have been possessed of some mighty Sound, because I never forgot it and I was only 4-and-three-quarters years old.

This Radio Sound was, of course, American commercial AM radio through a variety of mostly small speakers, monophonic and full of "atmospherics," as Major Armstrong, self-defenestrated inventor of FM, would say. And yet this Sound was mesmerizing.

Mesmerizing, too, in my Los Angeles teens, were Gilbert & Sullivan operettas on Sunday mornings, played from many sides of heavy London 78s spinning at classical KFAC; Rhythm and Blues from a record shop at 120th and Central — "Huntin' with Hunter" Hancock on weeknights; Holy Roller sermons from Downtown churches on Sunday; the Frost Warnings interrupting the first five minutes of *Suspense* when the orange groves began to freeze in January; Summer broadcasts of Gershwin and the 1812 Overture with real cannons from the Hollywood Bowl.

And all of this, all of these voices and personalities and pop, classical, R&B, Chet Huntley with the News, Amos and . . . , Blondie and . . . , George and . . . , Fibber McGee and . . . , Mr. and . . . (comedy duets by the first and best writers in the "situation" form), all these came into my ears yes, in mono and from small speakers, entirely "brought-to-you-by" and slightly out of tune.

It also arrived in the Sound ambience of my room, or the living room (before TV), or the kitchen, or the car. The Sound waves traveled through the air I breathed, and so the Sounds themselves tasted of the sights and smells of Life.

Anything and everything more in the realm of sound is the result of tsunami technology. Technology, and being at the right place at the right time, allowed me to participate in some of those moments when the hardware, software and brain-ware get to kick in, add some Hertz, more tracks, a lot of channels, chips that approach infinity — a longer, wider, deeper reaching into the Moreness of Sound.

When I first got over to the other side — the other Sound — of Radio and became a — what? — a DJ, a combo-operator, an FM announcer and program host, a voice like those I listened intently to when Old Radio's heart was still pumping — when I was on the In-Side of Sound, then the ambience shifted. Some Sounds were never to be heard on the Outside — the backward-playing half-spin of an LP to cue it up; the station phone ringing just before the moment to turn the announce pot up; the Klezmer band recording in the little studio and coming through the newscast on the air; suppressed coughs, the occasional giggle and the tick of the Western Union clock.

This was FM radio just beginning, really, and I passed my announcer's test reading — "announcing" — random selections from the shelves of the music library — Brahms and Shostakovitch and Dvorak and boxes of all the Bachs with notes in German. *On Your Toes*, or maybe it was *Oklahoma* or Oscar Brand, maybe movie music or the Modern Jazz Quartet's new "Pyramid."

WBAI in 1959 played just about anything and had a schedule full of live, personality-driven programs — a luncheon show with tall, blonde folksinger Cynthia Gooding and a succession of anemic males known as "Sensible"; Jonathan Schwartz beginning his radiophonic affair with Frank Sinatra (he's still at it now, somewhere in New York, New York). And Miles Krueger, historian of American Musical Theatre, armed with 78s from the 1920s, which he kept stored in bookcases that once belonged to Richard Rodgers.

After 1960, when WBAI was given to the Pacifica Foundation, as a valuable addition to their famously leftist station in Berkeley and the new outlet in Los Angeles, our little studio in New York played host to Pauline Kael and Alan Watts, to Peter Ustinov, who adlibbed a Bach Oratorio, singing all the parts; to Irish playwright Brendan Behan, who had very soft little hands. Also, we let the Communist Party USA edit a broadcast of their 1960 Convention in our studio, all of them looking like and probably being FBI agents. I recorded Mae Murray, silent film queen, yellow-haired, bee-stung lips, and all in pink silk; assisted John Cage and David Tudor, who randomly created an entirely I Chingish assemblage of all manner of recorded sounds from three different turntables while reciting epigrams and Zen-ish surrealities.

Finally, in 1961, my first feature documentary based on 40 weeks of interviews with and readings by the new, hot post-Beat poets and international little magazine editors. All literary voices practicing what Dylan Thomas named "The Sullen Art." I was now what the BBC would call a Features Producer and I was learning the craft from the many BBC Transcriptions which we played. (The BBC also offered *The Goon Show*, which became a primary radiophonic influence on the nascent Firesign Theatre.)

As I was learning broadcasting, LPs were changing the way long-form jazz, classical and the incoming psychedelic sides were played and programmed on the air. Stereo was on its way to add a second layer to LPs and forthwith to radio. As a matter of fact, WBAI was the left side of the first stereo broadcast in New York City. Yes, you needed two radios, three feet apart, one tuned to us, one to WRVR up at the Riverside Church where the concert was taking place.

In our studio, Ampex 350s spooled pancakes of Scotch quarter-inch recording tape easily edited with an aluminum block, sharp razorblade and some gummy mending tape laid down with a deft flick of the blade and smooth pressure of the thumb.

These first couple of years on the inside side of the Radio transformed my notion of what the outside sound of Radio could, should and, if I could help it, would be. A hotbed of the unexpected.

The early Sixties began the time to take over the Sound of Radio, play with it, experiment with it, use it to capture History instead of reproduce recordings, use it to stay just over the edge of what smart New Yorkers, far-flung Angelinos, and hipster-pacifist Berkeleyites might need to hear. The three Pacifica stations in the Sixties and Seventies were home to most of the engineering, production and on-air talents of the far-flung NPR Empire of the Eighties at the beginning of their public radio careers.

In the late 1960s, in Southern California, the transformation of Sound on the air exploded with The Beatles, Rock 'n' Roll and the War. I and my partners in the Firesign Theatre, led by senior partner Peter Bergman and his *Radio Free Oz* program, invaded LA airspace with unrehearsed put-on riffs, ragas by East Indians, prophesy from American Indians, and Peter's own personality, which absorbed every author he chose to read aloud to his just-getting-stoned constituency, with the result that Peter became whoever they thought he was. This kaleidoscopic identity-shifting was a gift of radio and we took advantage of it.

The Firesign spent the Summer of Love writing and recording four long sketches for our first LP — "Waiting for the Electrician or Someone Like Him." The album was constructed out of true-life-adventures; found ephemera, our recent radio documentary work with the Hopi, random encounters with the principal figures of the hallucinogenic moment and their worshipers, bits of Beckett, Ionesco and the Spike Milligan. Sgt. Pepper meets The Mothers of Invention. The interesting idea of a record as more than a surface or a medium — a dimension. On Side Two we welcomed our hopefully disoriented listeners to Side Five and began a Turkish language lesson.

Firesign began recording inside the studios formerly inhabited by the CBS Radio Network near Sunset and Vine. Studio A, soon to become a vast TV Newsroom, had been a thousand-seat auditorium for the likes of Jack Benny. Studio B was the location for *Suspense*, and the art-deco glass window of the director's booth was still in place and proved to be a groovy place to hang out during our Union engineers' coffee breaks.

Four-track machines allowed us to separate and place voices in the stereo field, to lay half-a-dozen sound effects and music tracks down, mix them down, massage them. We even recorded outside the building, banging on a VW Bug and screaming for a dose of the plague. The result was an album with a Sound you had to, wanted to, listen to more than once. An album meant to sit on the same shelf with "Rubber Soul," "Highway 61," "Absolutely Free" and, shortly destined to spawn an act that played on the same stages as Ravi Shankar, Buffalo Springfield and Taj Mahal.

In the fall of 1967, *Radio Free Oz* found itself on KRLA, an AM outlet with a huge reach in the L.A. Basin. We did 13 weeks of Firesign sketches, broadcasting our surrealist *Goon Show*-inspired takes on old educational films, pirates, Sherlock Holmes, Robin Hood and Ancient Rome — what a circus! The Sound of the Past in the City of the Future.

❖❖❖

A lot of folks wanted to get in on the concept comedy album after Firesign's second LP — "How Can You Be in Two Places at Once," backed on Side 2 with "Nick Danger" — but record companies were less interested in that idea than they had been three years before and the doors only opened for a few writer/audio producers and then closed pretty tightly on the second generation of post-radio audio playwrights, many of whom had been inspired to begin playing with Sound by the Firesign's model.

Both "Nick" and "How Can You Be" were meant to mimic the sounds of American radio and Golden Age pop culture. "Nick" was based on an amalgam of radio heroes, his criminal nemesis Rocky on the immortal Peter Lorre. Sgt. Bradshaw is a familiar tough-guy character from film and radio (Lloyd Nolan, maybe), and the fourth person (me), playing both the Butler and the Announcer, is instrumental in exposing and destroying, one by one, the unmentionables of Golden Age Radio studio technique. Nick imagines — creates — the ambience and the sound effects as he goes along, telling his tattered tales. A closet full of old RCA radio mikes, the studio Hammond organ, and a few leftover CBS sound props gave Radio authenticity to our Sound, complete with the punctured fourth wall that all radio comedy naturally worked with, adding that comical layer of surreal self-consciousness.

With HCYB, we were finally free, with eight tracks open to us, to create a set of ambiences and listening experiences to make a movie-in-your-mind of being in two-places-at-once with our Hero, Babe, who buys a new RV from a TV pitchman, drives it onto the Xeno's Paradox Freeway off ramp, on which Time slows, casting him somehow onto the stage of a great American Pageant, as it might have been created by Norman Corwin, had he been writing for the Marx Brothers and W.C. Fields.

Poor Babe is drafted — is it 1944 or 1969? — and sent off to Bring the War Back Home with all the cheap glamour Paranoid Pictures could afford to buy. And, as the movie ends and the TV station goes off the air, the CHANNELS SWITCH! Bits, found fragments, words chopped out of the ethereal airwaves by the hand of the listener, who dreams that the TV pitchman, once a used-car huckster, now peddles pot and James Joyce androgynously on this channel, the one in stereo on your earphones, while you meditate on What Next?

DO — The Right Hand of OZ, KRLA, 1967

2. MAY I SEE YOUR PASSPORT PLEASE?
The first of four short introductory essays in The Firesign Theatre's Big Book of Plays. *Here began my attempt to focus attention on the seriousness of Firesign's purpose in creating these audio comedies. (1972)*

When we began the first album, the first thing we agreed to write about was the American Indian. It was not only the natural ground, the Ur-fact about life on the North American continent, but we had been tremendously impressed by the Hopi Prophesy and moved by a way-of-life which had long been maintained as a pure alternative to the one in which we found ourselves. So we wrote a history of the Indian and called it "Temporarily Humboldt County."

History lesson concluded, we found ourselves (as always) in the Present. It was Los Angeles and 1967, the Year of the Love-In. Marijuana was in every brownie, acid in every cup of punch and Sgt. Pepper on every turntable. What was happening? Was it Chocolate, Strawberry or W. C. Fields Forever?

Only the Future would tell. It was obvious that we were living through the beginnings of a Revolution, during which even the names of the months might be changed, as in 18th-century France. So we projected ourselves as far as we could — all the way to the literary end of our "War in Nigeria" on the 38th day of Cunegonde.

Thus, America's Past, our Present, and that vision of the Present which we call "Future." When we had written these three short pieces, we turned to a longer work, something we knew we were going to call "Waiting for the Electrician or Someone Like Him" even before we realized that its subject matter was Power. Because things already seemed to be well underway, we began on Side Five with a language lesson and a character called "P" (because Phil played the part, and in homage to Kafka's Josef K.).

So it is that "P" finds himself getting off an airplane (the *Enola McLuan?*) in the dangerously neutral countries of "Enroute," from which escape seems impossible. His identity is put in question; he is deliberately isolated and harassed. He cannot understand the language or where he is being sent. He arrives late, of course, to a gathering in the honor of a dying War Hero. He escapes the revolutionary holocaust which follows, receives instruction in

Command and, from his underground post in the Generator Room (as close to The Grid as one can safely get), he takes over.

No sooner has he done so but he is thrown into prison, where his aged alter-ego and a host of faceless prisoners try to make him see the hopelessness (and stupidity) of his position. Faced with an electrical death sentence, "P" reverts to childhood and wakes from his nightmare on the stage of a TV quiz show. He has been here before, too! Back now, once again, to try and find out what it is that's killing him. It's The Plague! Everybody wants it! It's what's happening! "P" makes a final desperate dash for safety and is picked up by a friendly cabdriver — a driver who seems to be an agent for another unnamed Power.

"P," on orders from the driver, shucks off his clothes — his contagion — and throws them to the ravening crowd. The cab smashes through the border crossing, and just as the whole cycle begins again (for beyond every border lies another country Enroute) someone who knows how pulls the plug. The cycle is broken.

3. REVOLUTIONARY RECORD, OR WHAT GOES AROUND COMES AROUND

Written for the first CD release of "Waiting for the Electrician or Someone Like Him." I arrived at the conclusion that this LP was unquestionably the most important literary achievement of the alternative movement of the late 1960s. (1991)

Here are a couple of stories I've heard . . .

When "Waiting for the Electrician or Someone Like Him" arrived at WBAI in New York City, Bob Fass played it on his show, *Radio Unnamable*, over and over, all night, first side one, then side two, then side one, then side two, then side five . . . The next day the Whole Town Was Talking . . .

A portable stereo blasted "Electrician" onto the rooftop of a downtown Saigon hotel during the Tet Offensive, while a gaggle of stoned newsmen stood around listening and watching bomb bursts and artillery flashes in the suburbs . . . The record had been bought at the PX . . .

Not to mention that in 1968 my back-door neighbor, David Grimm (who went on briefly to be Nick Danger's organist), offered any visitor to his humble cottage the opportunity to drop acid, watch Super 8 home movies projected onto Janis Joplin posters and listen to "Electrician," through earphones, very loud . . . Many of his visitors did many of those things (if not all at once . . .).

A quarter of a century ago, when the four young men who wrote and performed this record album were known (if only to themselves) as the "Oz" Firesign Theatre, radio had suddenly, thanks to rock 'n' roll, become a revolutionary force and a direct channel of communication to youth, to the anti-war movement, to the immerging counter-culture. This seizure of the ether happened on both coasts and at various temporarily "safe" undergraduate havens in between.

In LA, the big rockers KMET and KRLA finally got themselves "hippified" in time for the Summer of Love, but where it all started was KPFK, when Peter Bergman arrived on a late-night motorcycle in the Spring of '66, fresh and flowery from Berlin and Turkey, with his own 16mm movie, starring his own bald self, stuck in his pack. Within a few months half the town had joined "The Wizard" on his late-night phone-in rap-time psyche-trip, *Radio Free Oz*.

The three of us who were around at the right time (the Summer of 1967) to make a record with the Famous Peter Bee, an album based on the new kind of comedy we had been creating for "Oz," were Phil Proctor — a musical comedy juvenile from Yale with a trick for falling off couches and possibly a promising future in films; a cheerful KPFK announcer-producer and good-looking Hollywood hopeful named Phil Austin; and yours truly, a "published poet," and former radio personality, just over the hill at 30 and about to Drop Out in a big way. Our photos were, I guess for recorded history, pasted on the album cover in a "naive collage," all over an old print of bored Indians being preached at by a now four-headed orator. Probably he, or we, is (or am) *not* The Electrician, for whom, possibly we are all still waiting.

❖❖❖

"Waiting for the Electrician or Someone Like Him" is the first in a series of albums by the Firesign based on the traditions of radio theatre — audio drama, "ear-plays," movies-for-your-mind — and the classic formats of Broadcasting's Golden Age, then only a decade or so gone.

Being the first album, it is probably the most astonishing. It is as *noir* as Lenny Bruce, as hip as Lord Buckley, as full of funny voices as Stan Freberg. It does for the tie-die T-shirt what Newhart did for the button-down collar, but it has more in common with Redd Foxx than with Shelley Berman. It is Sgt. Pepper multi-tracked with *The Lone Ranger, Gangbusters* and *Hear It Now!* It takes our childhood memories of radio as a powerful stimulus to our imaginations and surrealizes them into a form you can take home and listen to again and again.

It has to be the bleakest comic portrait of America since *Huckleberry Finn*. The first three cuts take care of our Past, Present and Future. The neolithically traditional Hopilanders are shown to be war-painted movie extras. The Paisley Gurus of the moment reveal themselves to be power-freaks who claim the Sunrise for their own special-effect. The Post-Revolutionary Hippy Hegemony and Soul Brotherhood Police State gives away free food and the President sings Motown, but he'd rather hit you with a book than let you read one.

The quotable quips are endless: "This is our sacred antenna." "It's a beaut'." "No, it's a mound." "Just what you need for a better education — French horn, Italian, water polo." "Say, man . . . got any pie-oh-tee?" "Scalpum, Tantric!" "Ranger's on a bum trip again." "Meditate on the pure white light of stupidity." "He's groovy. All spades are groovy." "Take him away for Re-er-Grooving!" And what great sounds! A hydrogen bomb blast, a huge toke, a horse that snorts LSD and turns into a fundamentally better elephant, the *Enola McLuan* cruising over rebel Nigeria.

I freely admit that parts of "Temporarily Humbolt County" virtually segue from Freberg's "United States of America," and that Gary Usher's production sometimes makes us sound like we're still overdubbing Chad and Jeremy's "Progress Suite." And it could be that "W. C. Fields Forever" owes something to Peter Sellers' audio travelogue "Balham — Gateway to the North." The bag lady with the faded San Francisco art-nouveau body paint may quote Allen Ginsberg's "Howl" as proof of Groovy-ness in the best-of-all-possible neon nights of "Le Treint-Huite Cunegonde," but this final chapter is an otherwise original mix of "Marat/Sade" and Ed Murrow from Hell. The entire "side" of the album becomes one non-linear drama, commencing with desert wind and native song and concluding with the relentless, familiar drone of a B-29 . . .

Have you heard? The word is "love" . . .

Something was happening, but it wasn't happening to you yet, was it Mr. or Ms. Jones? Not until you played Side Five. Not until you arrived at the Turkish Border . . . "Is *this* your bar of soap?"

The theme is Power. Power and Death. The stuff of great comedy. Kafka's K. as filmed by Welles. Beckett's Existential Clowns as observed by Hitchcock. Brecht's sinister underworld adapted by Kubrick. A Modernist Satire of the Rise to Leadership, ending with the rim shot clang of a Warner Bros. prison door. Fred Astaire tap dances on the telephone. The Electrician waits by his Chair. Then, the twist!

You, thanks to TV, now viral with the Plague, you, Mr./Ms. Black Death, you have become just what everyone wants — the contagious object of desire, pursued, taxi-ing away from the dying who sing by the riverside, tearing off your infectious clothes, crashing across another Border just in time for coffee and a sweet. It's all a B-movie . . . a bum trip . . . a nightmare . . . pull the plug on it . . . Death to Power . . .

Chronologists have a hard time placing The Firesign Theatre. "Jesters for the Rock Generation." "The Marx Brothers of the Sixties." "A notorious early-'70s counter-culture audio-theatre satirical troupe." Let it be explained here that "Electrician" is an album of the Sixties. If there had been no more from us, "Electrician" would still sum up Amerika as of that historic summer. And it's still pure Underground Radio. Tune in and pump up the volume!

Remember, what ya don't mean won't hurt ya . . .

4. STILL WAITING, OR SOMETHING LIKE IT
NOTES FROM THE SUMMER OF LOVE
A third look at "Electrician" and a closer one at the day-to-day creative process behind the writing of this album. Research for a 1992 radio documentary. (1997)

Here's more-or-less how it all started, as we moved from FM to AM, via Hopiland, Elysian Park and the forgotten CBS Radio studios on Sunset Blvd.

MARCH: According to my 1967 UNICEF calendar, the Firesign's year started on Sunday, March 12, with the "Indian Documentary" on *Radio Free Oz*. I'm supposing now that that broadcast was the final installment of our month-long series — an original radio play by Phil Austin called "A Shadow Falls Upon the Land." (I had previously done a historical piece with many readings from the actual words of both Native Americans and Injun-haters, and Peter Bergman had produced a visionary program on Indian prophecies, based on our warmly remembered Winter Solstice visit to the Hopis.)

My week included a gathering of the "tribes" at the *Oracle* office on Fairfax Boulevard. I was then the poetry editor of the Southern California edition of that famed San Francisco psychedelic tabloid. I was also teaching a poetry workshop at the Westside Community Center and my calendar shows frequent meetings during the year with various writers around town. On Saturday, March 18, Peter hosted the Oz Indian Colloquium, which was a gathering of the "tribes" for sure. Fringy leather jackets and turquoise jewelry made their first appearance in Southern California.

On Easter Sunday, March 26, came the first Love-In, advertised over KPFK by all four of us. Peter and I spent much of the day in a teepee in Elysian Park, amid the jangle of bells and a pounding surf of drums.

That was the way it began, with real Indians — traditional Third Mesa Hopis — and would-be Indians. With poets and hipsters and potheads and hippies — and these were the first ingredients to be stirred into the recipe for "Electrician." Craig Carpenter, our "faithful Indian compendium," supplied the title for the album's first cut when he declared "Temporarily" Humbolt County, California was over-due for a name-change back to whatever the original inhabitants had called it.

APRIL: We were working at both KRLA, our new AM mega-watt playground, and at non-commercial KPFK. After I got back from a week in Ohio judging underground movies at Kenyon College, the Firesign made its first in-person appearance at UCLA (on the 28th). Peter had billed us as the Bulgarian National Theatre in Exile and we sullenly performed "Waiting for the Electrician." Or something somewhat like it.

MAY: I noted an evening rehearsal at Peter's on the first of the month, followed by a couple of midnight recording sessions at Columbia Records — the old CBS studios on Sunset Boulevard, still hardly altered from the heyday of network radio. These sessions most likely were when the first recording work was done on the "Electrician" album. The rest of the month found me spending weekends selling Lemon Delights at the Renaissance Pleasure Faire, reading my poetry to various audiences, recording at KPFK, meeting with Indians and continuing with midnight Firesign writing and recording sessions. Surely we were then working our way through "Temporarily Humboldt County" and "W. C. Fields Forever."

SUM-SUM-SUMMERTIME: Peter left for Turkey to do research on a screenplay. Lucky dog, riding high. The Phils and I did the KRLA Sunday Oz show for the next two months. Proctor telephoned in reports from the Monterey Pop Festival and I took time out to visit San Francisco over the Summer Solstice and listen to Big Brother and Jefferson Airplane. The anti-war movement was getting bigger all the time and I was there for the Angry Arts poetry reading at the Ashgrove. The Revolution was beginning and soon we would be celebrating its triumph — on the 38th of Cunegonde. On June 29, the Phils and I did voices for a Chad and Jeremy album. Several more sessions at Columbia show up on my calendar in mid-July. On August 4 the Hollywood Bowl played host to a program of Indian music, and about that time we might have done some recording on a cut we soon dropped from the album — a take-off on Ravi Shankar. Peter returned and we were all back at work at CBS on August 22.

SEPTEMBER: On the 9th Peter and I hosted a memorable concert of Indian music at the Pilgrimage Theatre, across the Hollywood Freeway from the Bowl. Did I play Ali Ali Infree? Oh my goodness gracious yes. By this time we've surely started to write and record "Side Five" of "Electrician." Not surprisingly, we began in the language (Turkish) out of which Peter had just reemerged.

Studio sessions continued for a final week in mid-September. *Radio Free Oz* went back on the air on the 10th, now "live" from the Magic Mushroom — an alcohol-free rock club on Ventura Boulevard — and soon would feature a full half-hour original comedy by the Firesign every week. Donovan played the Mellow Yellow Hollywood Bowl on September 23, and we auctioned off an autographed banana on the following night's broadcast.

OCTOBER: From the beginning of the month, the Firesign boys were holed up in an editing room at CBS finishing the album and, alternatively, writing furiously at Jeremy Clyde's Encino estate (where Proctor had taken up residence), fueled by a substance known as "Icebag." We also scheduled meetings with our lawyer and a man from William Morris. An audition was set for the Firesign on an upcoming Oz show.

Nineteen Sixty-seven ended with a regular schedule of four days a week of group writing (we had an office at CBS by this time) before each Sunday night live broadcast. We had become a fixture on the L.A. radio landscape, although we were to broadcast our last show in early January. The "Electrician" album was scheduled for release in March. We were set to open with unknown comedian Steve Martin at the Pasadena Ice House. And so, in fear and hot water, The Firesign Theatre was born.

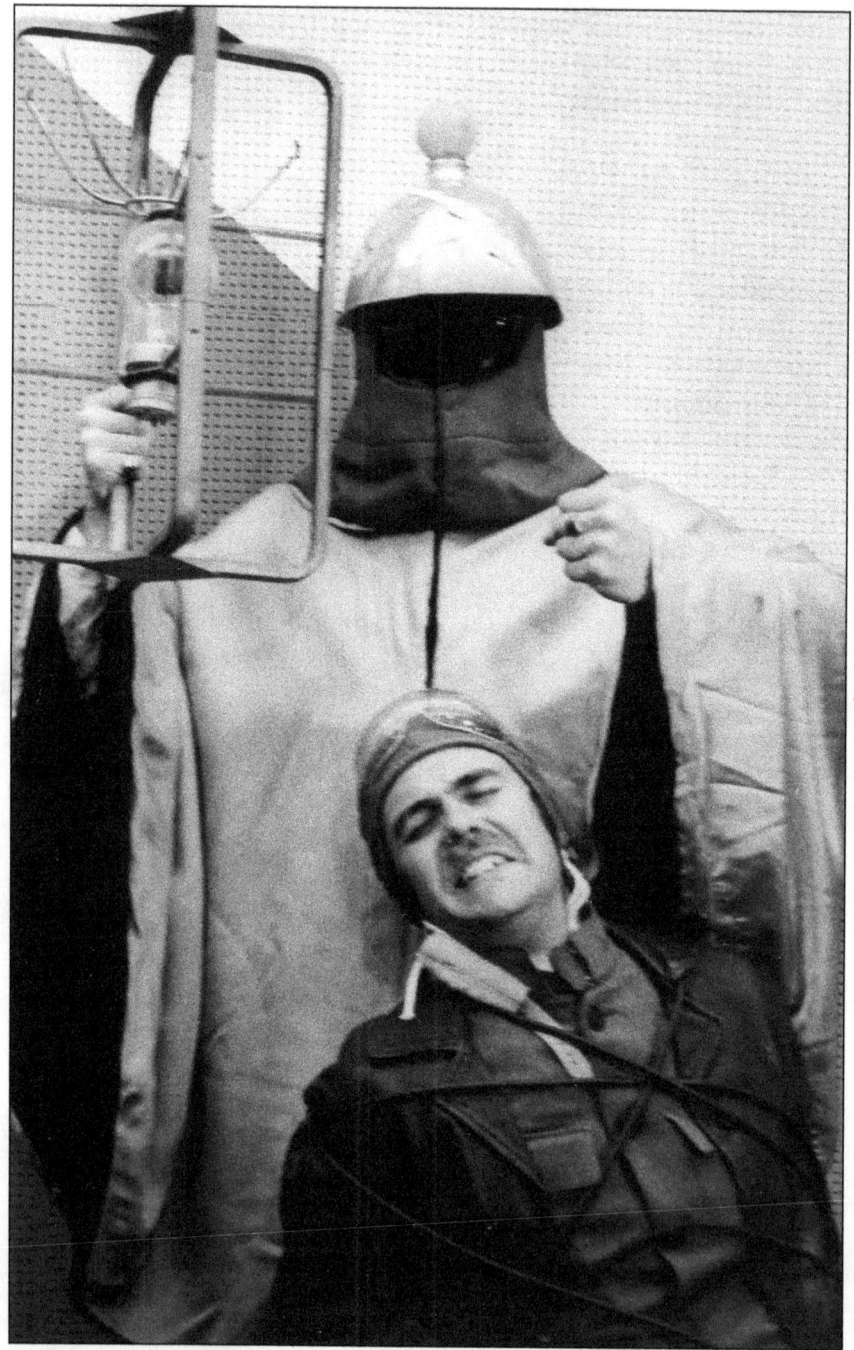

No Longer Waiting For the Electrician!
(Phil Proctor as "Frank Acne Jr." menaced by DO as "The Electrician")

5. WELCOME TO SIDE SIX

I continue to try to pull the "classic" Firesign albums into a single story. An Odyssey. From Homer to Joyce, this primal voyage home — an epic adventure told in poetic metaphor — was at the creative heart of Firesign's own unconscious epic. (1972)

The starting point was the Ralph Williams Mantra. Ralph live. Ralph on TV. Ralph on the AM and the FM. Ralph in Mexico, Moscow and Paris! A dubbed Italian adventure movie running underneath the whole thing.

Then came the Car itself. It was a used 1984 Nark Avenger, but it had a Trip-Master tape cartridge that not only told you where you were and where you were going, but introduced the parts of the engine in music and song, like an "educational" children's record.

Unfortunately, the musical extravaganza so confused the car's driver that he took the wrong off-ramp and ran out of gas on an old back road. The Trip-Master abandoned him with a warning to turn on his Climate Control and wait for help.

Under the spell of a Tropical Downpour, the driver fell asleep and into a delirious dream of Traveling . . .

This was the original beginning of "How Can You Be in Two Places at Once When You Aren't Anywhere at All." It was as if the character "P" had come running across The Border and had escaped, only to find himself on Ventura Boulevard in Encino. His new name was "Babe" and his odyssey continues with the act of buying a car "to get away from it all."

In the recorded version, Babe falls asleep in his car and finds himself stranded in the woods where a strange crew of "little men" (Gremlins? Dwarfs? Leprechauns?) pop up inside his head. They taunt him, and make terrible sport of him, and do W. C. Fields imitations and bad puns. The only way out of this dream seems to be through a frightening black hole that opens into . . . a tomb? A pyramid? The Great Seal of the United States?

But it turns out to be a Motel, for where else would a weary traveler go when he's been driving all day and it's been raining and he's sleepy? This Motel, however, has a couple of drunken conventioneers on hand to greet Babe, and they know who he really is. He's an American!

So the inspiring story of America and its people is performed for and with Babe, in a style partly borrowed from the patriotic radio and stage pageants that the WPA did so stirringly in the 1930s. But when the 1940s rolled around, so did the caissons; and so, of course, Babe's fate is to be drafted into that great equalizer of minorities, the US Army.

Or is it Babe's fate? Possibly he has drifted into another dream while watching an old movie on the car's TV — a movie called *Babes in Khaki*, in which the War is Brought Back Home. But the movie is finally over, and it's Late Late. Once through the dial, where that dubbed Italian movie about Ulysses is playing again (still?) and where Ralph sponsors everything.

Time to have a little toke and drift back into sleep . . .

6. ON BEING IN TWO PLACES AT ONCE

A fond memory of a terrible time. In 1968 to be truly American was to be Un-American. The nation was turned on its head. Firesign pulled it together to do a second, nearly hour-long LP, creating pieces we perform to this day. (1998)

It is April 25, 1968. Less than a month since Johnson withdrew from the race. Three weeks since King was killed. Bobby is running hard. The war has been really terrible — Tet, the battle for Hue, Westmoreland on TV, the talk about peace talks, napalm, helicopters. The young Firesign Theatre is about to open a rear guard action at a movie house called the Hilltop Theatre, way behind God's back in Tujunga, California.

The two Phils, Peter and I, have changed into our costumes for "The Giant Rat of Sumatra" in the two-chair barbershop next door to the theatre. We've run our lines for "The Indian Piece," nervously. Peter and I are now in the concrete exit corridor to the left of the movie screen waiting out the closing scenes of *Fahrenheit 451*. We are double-billed with the picture this week (next week we'll be replaced by The Marquis Chimps), and we are dying. There are ten people in the house and we are related to most of them.

Poised to enter, Peter whispers to me, "I've been thinking about our next album. We should call it "How Can You Be in Two Places at Once, When You're Not Anywhere at All." He sings it in a little jingle, like he does on the record.

"No, that's too long, Pete," I say. "Besides, what does it mean?"

September. Three months since they got Bobby. That leaves Humphrey and Rockefeller and Nixon and Wallace. We are back in the old CBS radio studios in Hollywood, recording the Second Album, and we make the candidates' names into a locomotive that rolls over The Little Guys. The album, which started out with Ralph Williams and LA's obsession with vee-hickles, takes a left turn into the "tropical paradise" of Vietnam. America's obsession. Winning hearts and minds. Strategic hamlets. Body bags.

In a parody of those half-forgotten Norman Corwin World War II time radio pageants we paint new-car-buyer Babe with blackface and draft him. Better some of him than some of us! With The Whole World Watching, we Bring the War Back Home (where it ought to have been before!). Yes, Dear Friends, the President of the United States is named Schicklegruber.

Reaching for *Ulysses*, we free-associate with James Joyce to fashion a coda for our American Comedy. Click. Click. Through the channels of the mind toward the message, "Yes. Yes. It's gonna be all right! Yes." We croon this from the stage often over the next few years.

Nixon. Nixon in November. The casualty figures are always rising. Astronaut heroes reach very close to the Moon. More heart transplants. The White Album is out, and John Wesley Harding. The year turns to 1969. "Sixty-nine" thumbs its nose from souvenir T-shirts and football jerseys. Revolution is fashionable. The Red Guards are busy.

Peter and I are on KMET Sunday mornings, reading from books and spinning our musical picks. We think of Oz as a Religious Program and we preach from the Bible, Castaneda and Winnie-the-Pooh. Revelations. Birthdays. Rebirthdays.

Together again, the Firesign Boys fashion a pilot radio program for Jack Poet Volkswagen, part of which ends up on Side Two of the Second Album when we get fired from the show before we even do it. A slightly dope-crazed parody of a radio dick. Magically, a classic. Nick, on the radio, in two places at once, blends right into, even through, the plastic. This side comes with funny voices that anybody can do, about 30 Secret Beatles References, a real CBS door, old RCA mikes, David Grimm on the Hammond electric, and contains the Secret of Radio: all you have to do to make a tough transition is fade your voice out and cue the organist. Yep. Never fails. Thanks, Nick.

Nick's LA has sure changed. I sometimes still see the lettering on his office window — REGNAD KCIN — in that rundown stucco building at Hollywood and Whitley, but the rural, ramshackle acres called The Farm, where Peter and Phil A. and our producer Cyrus Faryar lived, and where we wrote, recorded and made movies, across the road from Universal City, have been condos a long time now. And, yes, friends, this hand-painted, psychedelic VW Bug is not a collector's item, here, where the freeway murder of your choice is still in progress. Remember, Fantastic Cigarettes have gone to war under the Zero Tolerance edict.

But, as Dan Catherwood said, "Glad to have someone to talk to after all these years. Why don't we sing something?" Join me. I just hope you haven't forgotten the key.

7. "A LIFE IN THE DAY"

Again, in The Big Book of Plays, *I continue the Firesign Odyssey. "Don't Crush That Dwarf, Hand Me the Pliers" is Firesign at its collaborative best. The Unities of time, space and place nullified and deconstructed. The beginning of a new saga awakening from the dense language itself. (1972)*

In January 1968, we wrote the last script in a series of half-hour plays which we were performing on AM radio. It departed from the more absurd character-comedies we had been doing, being based on a day's television programming. Beginning with the morning's first show, "Today's Day Today," it continued (with commercial interruptions) with the day's broadcasts of "Sailor Bill," "The

End of the World," "Ozzie Knows Father," The Evening News" (including an item about a man-made baby), "The Golden Hind," and a Western called "Garbanza!" Late in the evening, the TV channels were changed, switching through several bits of programs, including an Italian movie and the Ralph Spoilsport-sponsored Late Late Show, *Babes in Khaki*. At last, after a prayer and the National Anthem, the station and the set were turned off for the day.

The concept of channel-switching stuck and, for "How Can You Be in Two Places at Once" we incorporated this idea, expanding on several of the original scenes and, in effect, making the Late Late Show the frame for the entire opus.

Mudhead & Porgie
Photo by Jonathan Perry

After the release of "How Can You Be" in 1969, we were scheduled to appear during Christmas week at the Ash Grove in Hollywood. For the date, we resurrected the radio script ("A Life in the Day" it was called) expanded on everything we hadn't used on record, clicking through many more channels and ending with the ever-popular Ralph Spoilsport Mantra. This is the piece we performed while on tour in the East in March 1970.

As the performances went on, "The TV Set" began to change. Someone would contribute a new character, commercial or TV show, from night to night. The new bits were pieced into the script, which got longer and longer. Somewhere along the line, Phil Austin brought in a teenage horror movie starring some well-known comic-book figures, and Peter introduced Mrs. Presky.

The new record was much on our minds during the Eastern tour. It had been decided that I would carry on the story of "P" and Babe, but the context remained hidden until we sat down at the round table after our return and started writing. It seemed sensible to begin by turning on the electricity and, in order to let everyone know that it was "going to be all right," our old friend Pastor Flash was summoned up from the Powerhouse Church.

The Pastor arrives in his mock B-29 (the *Enola McLuan?*) to the rousing strains of "Marching to Shibboleth," a song we had written to be sung in a movie called *Zachariah*. The movie we wrote was never made, perhaps luckily.

By the time Pastor Flash lands he is on all-night television.

If it was Babe who fell asleep watching Ralph, it is George Tirebiter who awakes at 4 AM, ravenously hungry. The TV drones on. The advertised food is not available in George's area. The Pizza Man is not there. But the Pastor offers his TV flock sustenance, material as well as spiritual. George falls for it, grabbing the glowing color-TV groat cakes right out of the tube and gorging himself on them.

The ingestion of this "food" works its changes on George, who suddenly becomes a character on the TV, moving through the TV world in several guises. He is, by turns, an old movie director, a political candidate, a child star, a high-school kid, an adult actor, an Army Officer, a quiz show MC. As George goes through his changes, the night world of the TV continues.

Someone (George himself?) switches through the channels, torn between watching "High School Madness!" and/or "Parallel Hell!" It is the black-and-white movie world of the 1950s where Authority Questioned is, or ought to be, Authority Triumphant. And inside of it, George is on trial because he (like the JDs Pico and Alvarado) ultimately refuses to believe what his Authority Figures tell him he must believe.

In the nick of time, as the movie-studio-world is being auctioned off around them, Tirebiter Man and Boy confront one another. Realizing that they are the same person, and that they have both "sold out," the Lieutenant walks out of his movie and George (with a four-letter word) drops his load out of the TV.

Pastor Flash's sermon is over. George, like Babe, seems to have fallen asleep watching the TV. Awakened, he clicks it off. The phone rings. During the long night, all the great comic spirits have called on him, the answering service reports. But George is still hungry. The sound of an ice-cream truck in the distance distracts him. He opens his door to find birds singing in the early morning. To be outside restores his youth and he runs after the bells, having escaped at last.

8. POWER IS TROUBLE AND TROUBLE'S NOT FUNNY

The Dear Friends *radio shows came in between albums and were broadcast nationally from a set of 12 LPs we sold to radio stations. A two-record set was put together from airchecks and old cassette recordings. This is the CD liner note. (1989)*

We were between records. Our first big tour and the album that followed — "Don't Crush That Dwarf, Hand Me the Pliers" — had filled the first half of 1970. In September we went back on the air from whence we had come — the studios of KPFK, Los Angeles' community radio station. We did twenty-one weekly shows between September 9, 1970 and February 17, 1971. Unlike *Radio Free Oz*, which had really been Peter's program, this was unmistakably One Hour with Us, with The Firesign Theatre, whatever that was. Whatever you heard was who we were at the moment.

We had virtually no scripts, mostly no plan of action. We brought into the studio what interested us; from the daily news, short bits we might have written, notebooks and sketchpads, a harmonica, a violin, and a squeaky pickle. We brought ourselves, wives, girlfriends, fans, a producer named Bill McIntyre, who tried hard to make sure we *Dear Friends* stayed on speaking terms with each other, and an engineer known as The Live Earl Jive, whose choices of music, sound effects and reverb were strictly his own. When the red light went on, so did we all.

After *Dear Friends* stumbled off the air, we wrote "I Think We're All Bozos on This Bus," and, in our spare time, put together a 12-record set of hour-long broadcasts, which we offered to the underground FM rockers. Only one hundred sets were pressed, and these are now among the rarest of Firesign artifacts. From those twelve hours, 74 minutes of short cuts were untimely ripped, in hopes that we would finally get some air time on stations unwilling to play an entire comedy album.

Now (1992), 21 years have passed. The Nix is still around, The Hoove is not. Big Boom-Boom Air Force Base has been shut down. Deputy Dan still has no friends. Giant Toads and Dukes of Madness have continued to arise on the Right. The Balliol Brothers hang around the stoplight on the Left. None of them will find this record funny. But then, being Power Hungry, they can't afford to find anything funny. I expect you can. And, fortunately for you, the CD format allows you to hear something like an original *Dear Friends* broadcast without flipping sides. A jagged rhythm of jokes, commercials, sketches, improvs, sermons, poems, laffs. Sudden riffs on language, lists of words, neighborhood dialects. Some whatchu-might-call "audio art." And so, Deeee-ar Frieeeends . . . press Play.

9. INTRAT ET EXIT UT NIL SUPRA!
Yes, it does. It goes in and out like anything! The fourth album had only been out a year or so when I wrote the final introduction for The Big Book of Plays. *At the time, Firesign's future was very much a clouded crystal ball. (1972)*

We had often talked about writing a children's record. Sometimes the talk concerned a record for children, but more often it was the form of a children's album which appealed to us. Before the writing of "Dwarf," we had discussed an album featuring a character called St. Beepo, the Macrocephalic Clown — an obvious ancestor of Barney Bozo. During September and October 1970 we had written a couple of false starts for an album to be titled "Why Does the Porridge Bird Lay its Eggs in The Air?," which starred various animal characters. Even earlier, we had outlined a kid's radio program called "The Whisperin' Squash Show," with a storyteller named Dr. Memory and an all-vegetable cast of cowboys and bad men.

When we started writing "I Think We're All Bozos on This Bus" on April 15, 1971, the manuscript was titled "Biting Through," after the hexagram we had thrown twice — once on the final day of "Dwarf" and again as we began work on the fourth album. Indeed, our character did seem to have "bitten through" — to have escaped into a world over which he could exercise some measure of personal control. Once again, we began by turning on the electricity. In this case, it was the electric typewriter which sat ready on the round table. The writing proceeded, serial-fashion, until the 23rd of June, interrupted by sessions in the studio in which we recorded what had been written to date. Always, the next episode in the story was unclear to us until the previous episode had been completely produced. The plot unwound as slowly as a mystery novel.

"Bozos" begins on the same street down which George Tirebiter had just pursued the ice-cream truck. Hunger satisfied, and with nothing else to do on a beautiful fall morning, George — now transmogrified into a young man named Clem — is amused and intrigued by the arrival of the Future Fair Tour Bus. He watches familiar cartoon characters invite him electronically aboard and, shoeless and carefree, decides to join the Bozos.

Inside the Bus, surrounded by an ever-changing synthetic environment, Clem and his seat-mate Barney are kept entertained by the electronic system which guides the Bus and the Fair itself.

Clem, not used to Bozoing about, leaves Barney and decides to take a ride through one of the Fair's main shows, The Wall of Science. The Wall submerges its viewers into an animated, multi-dimensional educational exhibit, in which they are treated to a History of Life, from Before the Beginning on through the Dawn of Man, the Age of Enlightenment and finally the Scientific Era.

At last, the Wall arrives at The Future itself. Government representatives now present Clem and the rest of the audience a dramatized lecture on the System, in order to prepare them for the Fair's biggest attraction, a personal visit with The President.

Each Fairgoer is treated to this realistic scene in turn and in each case The President speaks directly to the individual, attempting to answer each personal question. It is at this point that Clem, for reasons of his own, reprograms the system which controls the operation of the Fair and its many elements. He reaches deeply into the core of the system, but is unable to find the program which will answer the question he poses: "Why does the porridge bird lay its egg in the air?" In self-defense, the system shuts down The President and shunts off the audience to the Funway — a vast arena filled with noisy, diverting entertainment and crowds of gawking Bozos.

Clem, concerned that his connection with the broken ride will get him into trouble, joins Barney in an attempt to lose himself in the crowd. But, before they can get on one of the amusement cars, he is identified by one of the Fair's holographic sentinels. Fortunately, Clem knows enough to un-program the hologram of Artie Choke and to reprogram it in his own likeness. So doing, he creates his electronic double and sends it back into the system itself, where it searches through the machine's storage units to find the central memory core. The system resists the unauthorized (gypsy) program as best it can, but must finally check it out with the deepest cybernetic unit of all, the binomial duality known as Dr. Memory.

Clem's desperate program asks of Dr. Memory an unanswerable question. Confused, the Doctor is vulnerable and turns the entire machine off at its source. The Fair and all its creations vanish, leaving only the fireworks of its departure.

And now, the story changes. The Future is Past. And whose Future was it anyhow? We leave you to ponder this question, even as we are pondering it ourselves.

Shhhhhhhh! Quiet now! Here comes that little sailor . . .

10. WELCOME (TO THE FUTURE) BOZOS!

In this CD essay, I tried to render the carny atmosphere of "I Think We're All Bozos on This Bus" with a series of opening quotations. How much this album predicts, the Future is still coming true, of course, in a 21st century when politics and entertainment are both dominated by cartoons. (1989)

I. FOUR DEFINITIONS

BOZO: A man; fellow; guy; esp. a large, rough man or one with

more brawn than brains. 1934: "Drive the heap, bozo!" Chandler, Finger Man. From Sp. dial. "boso" (from "vosotros") = you (pl.) which resembles a direct address.
DICTIONARY OF AMERICAN SLANG by Wentworth and Flexner, 1960

BUS: A circuit in a mixing board which carries signals from one or more inputs to any output or set of outputs.
AUDIO CRAFT by Randy Thom, 1982

BARNY or BARNEY: In the English circus, a fight. The closest American equivalent is clem.

CLEM: Its most common meaning is that of a general fight or riot between town hoodlums who attack shows and the circus or carnival employees. As an interjection, clem has replaced Hey rube! as a battle cry for a forthcoming fight.
THE LANGUAGE OF AMERICAN POPULAR ENTERTAINMENT by Don B. Wilmeth, 1981

II. SOME FANCY RHETORIC
THEME OF FAIR IS SCIENCE

An epic theme! . . . Science discovers, genius invents, industry applies, and man adapts himself to, or is molded by, new things. . . . Individuals, groups, entire races of men fall into step with the slow or swift movement of the march of science and industry . . . "The Fair," wrote an observer, "considered as an electrical exposition only, would be well worth the attention of the world . . . It is barely within the compass of any man's mind to conceive of what the future has in store for us."
OFFICIAL GUIDE TO A CENTURY OF PROGRESS EXPOSITION, 1933

"THE WORLD OF TOMORROW MUST BE BUILT WITH THE TOOLS OF TODAY."

This is the gospel we feel you will be compelled to preach as you return thoughtfully from the Fair to your various destinations, filled, yes, and perhaps even overcome by the simple grandeur of

what you have seen, every bit of which tells you that a glorious future is at hand, that a new day, one in which mankind at last realizes the tremendous necessity for close cooperation, is dawning, and that science and industry will both serve you and in return demand your service, both simple and complex.
VIEWS OF THE NEW YORK WORLD'S FAIR, 1939

III. ON THE BUS AGAIN

. . . Garrison Keillor . . . world's tallest radio humorist . . . was drawn to the Eastern part of the U.S., he said. In the meantime, Denmark, where he was "just another bozo on the bus," would be his home.
TIME, *June 29, 1987*

We were on tour, three-dimensionally staging Clem's assault on Dr. Memory and "the breaking of the 'Resident," while the Nixon-Agnew Presidency was collapsing in showers of TV confetti in motel rooms coast-to-coast. It was the spring of 1974. We had written BOZOS three years before and now borrowed its general form as "second act" for the touring show, called ANYTOWN USA — A GUIDED TOUR THROUGH FIRESIGN WORLD.

The first act of ANYTOWN, like side one of BOZOS, was shaped as a series of dioramic, holographic, Disneyland-ish carnival rides. On stage we performed favorite chunks from our first three albums, leading into the intermission with our famous parody (by Phil Proctor's Ralph Spoilsport) of Molly Bloom's "yes I will yes" erotic fantasy from James Joyce's ULYSSES. On the album, the main ride had been drawn from images suggested by Norman Bel Geddes' 1939 "Futurama" — an audio trip through the idyllic, plexiglassed, Art Deco City of the (1960) Future, fantasized in model form as a smog-free and regularly-intersected paradise for the internal combustion engine — and the 1933 H(W)all of Science building, which visitors entered "to marvel at the interpretations of science it offers."

Incidentally, the 1933 Chicago Fair also gave us both the "Bozo" (a fire-breathing dragon of a roller-coaster which "takes us for a ride in the manner of Jonah") and the "Bus" (a miniature Greyhound for carting visitors between the exhibit buildings) of the title, as well as such key suggestions as the "rocket cars" of the Sky Ride, the mechanical mammoths and cave-men of The World A Million Years Ago, a "heart-gripping" reproduction of Abe Lincoln's Birthplace, giant toys and Oz figures, and the entire pleasure-centered Mid(Fun)way.

In 1974 we had the opportunity, in the person of Phil Proctor, to amplify and develop Clem's personality and his reasons for trying to invade the memory banks of the Hal-like computer masterminding the Future Fair. Phil's stage monologues developed this story: Clem, a shoeless computer programmer for the Fair, was fired after he reprogrammed the Ralph Spoilsport Speedway ride to "smoke dope," i.e., slow down, free-associate, play. He has now reentered the Fair and broken into the maintenance circuits of "Dr. Memory" in order to reprogram it to "forget the past." As on the album, he succeeds in confusing the good Dr. into contradictory on/off instructions which sabotage the machine and destroy the fantastic illusions we had all taken for Reality.

Forgetting the Past edits and erases (like the gap in the Nixon Tapes) the Memory of the Future. Pay no attention to the gang behind the curtain at your peril, dear listeners.

The recorded ending of BOZOS leaves us behind as gypsy fortune-tellers, segueing into our next adventure. On stage, three years after, we vanished Dr. Memory's compelling fantasies with a flash-pot. The show was really "just them boys, foolin' around" with a long-abandoned main-frame. A caretaker chases the hackers out and pulls the chain on the last work-light.

BOZOS came at the end of the Firesign Theatre's first, "Sixties" creative manifestation. No use waiting for the Electrician anymore — he come an' he gone. The Seventies produced new illusions — Self, Sex and Psychic Phenomena — and everything we knew was proved wrong. When the Firesign "boys" enlisted in the Eighties as Fighting Clowns, they sang "Everyone's a Bozo on this Bus/Zips and Beaners sittin' next to us/Are you a hostage? Are you a spy?/Or just some Berserker who's prepared to die?" Now, just in time for the Nineties, with Berliner Walls and blindfolds falling, here's another chance to go back Before the Beginning, plug into the bus, honk a few nozos and remember the Future with a few old friends. Welcome aboard!

"The TV Set"

11. THE MARTIAN SPACE PARTY DIARY
A Chronicle of The Firesign Theatre, January-June 1972

Thanks to daybooks, diaries and calendars, I kept a pretty good record of this half-year in the life of Firesign. It's still hard to figure out why we sort of self-destructed after only five years together, but the record is clear. We had survived '68. Would we survive '72? (1996)

PROLOGUE

We had reached a creative peak in the spring of 1971 with the creation of our fourth album, "I Think We're All Bozos on This Bus." Soon after it was released that fall, we put together a double-album of short cuts from the "Dear Friends" radio broadcasts, a series which had frequently revv'd up our creative energies in the months before "Bozos" was produced.

We had been improvising together for years over the air, and it was now time for TFT to release a "comedy record" — one that maybe more FM stations would play. "Dear Friends" also turned out to be a multi-dimensional demonstration of TFT at work, and of our individual voices and styles.

In November 1971 we began a new series of live broadcasts on Thursday nights, again on KPFK, the L. A. Pacifica station where we four had met five years before on "Radio Free Oz."

Rolling Stone had profiled us in their September 30 issue. We were getting good airplay; the reviews of "Bozos" coming out everywhere were fantastic. CBS was advertising all four albums at once, available on LP, cassette and 8-track tape "For Berserkers, Zips & Bozos only!" TFT was finally making it.

After a short holiday hiatus we picked up the KPFK show again in January 1972 and also continued our regular L.A. meetings, usually at Phil Austin's great hillside house overlooking historic Mixville. I came down the coast from Santa Barbara for three or four days a week and usually stayed at the succulent-draped El Patio Motel in North Hollywood.

I kept a regular diary at that time which, along with other sources, makes up the following calendar of events: the story of THE MARTIAN SPACE PARTY, the last completed work, and the only film record of the Firesign's "Golden Age."

Sun 2 Jan 1972

DO's I Ching throw for "the new year of work" is The Well, changing to Obstruction. "The town can be changed, but the well cannot be changed. It neither increases nor decreases."

Mon 3 Jan

TFT meets at PA's and decides to work on "Anythynge You Want To," a long-contemplated Shakespeare parody, for the next album release (following "Bozos" and "Dear Friends").

DO sees *A Clockwork Orange*. "Images still in my head."

Tues 4 Jan

TFT meets at PA's with Alan Rinzler of Straight Arrow Press and sells the idea of the *Big Book of Plays*.

DO sees *Modern Times*.

Wed 12-Thurs 13 Jan
TFT meets in LA for radio show (the sixth in the live broadcast series, but not used for syndication).

Mariner 9 photos "Hint That Mars May Be 'Living.'" Grand Canyons and other vistas of Mars soon follow.

Tues 18 Jan
TFT has biz mtg about new CBS record contract.

DO meets with Steve Gillmor.

Thurs 20 Jan
TFT on radio with "very good show." (The first half-hour was released as the 4th in the syndicated series, "City O' Pigs," and the second part became show #5, "The Filipino Cheese-Ball War.")

Wed 26 Jan
DO sees *Carnal Knowledge*. "So-so."

Thurs 27 Jan
TFT on radio. "A great time." (We called it "Pastor Flash's Pirate Ministry of the Air," but didn't use the material in syndication.)

DO's super-8 movie, "Dear Friends," records TFT at work and play in January.

Tues Feb 1
DO writes a found soundpoem, "Time Capsules," for TFT's next show.

Hears "Bangladesh" album. DF album "not yet out."

Wed Feb 2
TFT meets with Steve Gillmor, who pitches himself to co-produce a film with TFT, financed with 5K front money from CBS.

DO watches opening ceremonies of Winter Olympics.

THURS FEB 4
   TFT's radio show "low key." (Called "The Harry Cox Show," this one was not edited for syndication, but yielded, as did others, material finally used in TFT's 1977 album, "Just Folks.")

SUN FEB 6
   TFT profiled in Sunday *New York Times*, headlined, "Why Do Kids Love These Four Zany Guys?"

WED FEB 9
   TFT writes "The Prologue Scene, beginning AYWT." (Actually, the shipboard scene, performed at the Martian Space Party.) "Dear Friends" has been released.

THURS FEB 10
   TFT writes "another 2 pages of AYWT." (The beginning of the Father's Ghost scene on Castle Pflegm's Battlements, also performed at MSP.)

   Radio show "better than the week before. Heavy on the Olympics, which we've been watching every night." (This show, the 10th in the series, became show #6 of the syndicated version — "The Underground Olympics.")

TUES FEB 15
   TFT meets, writes "one line in AYWT." (More, actually — the end of the Battlements scene.)

THURS FEB 17
   DO finishes "Year of the Rat." "Inspires PA to get out his guitar, teach PB to play the harp & generally to build a musical show." Show "a great success." Called "The Year of the Rat," this program introduced several characters later written into the MSP.

   Daily Variety announces TFT will be "launching a series of one-minute late-night TV spots, pitching Firesign Theatre's elpees," and notes that the last time CBS had bought TV time was for Donovan in 1968.

Sun Feb 20

DO watches "the Nix land in China" and edits five of the "Let's Eat!" radio shows for syndication.

Mon Feb 21

DO contemplates week to follow: "Last radio show coming up. TV ads in a week from today. More work on "Anything," plans for 3/30 show. Mtg with *Rolling Stone*, too!"

The Free University of the University of Maryland announces a course in "Advanced Firesign Theatre Interpretation."

Tues Feb 22

TFT meets. "Lots of the Phils playing music." SG in for mtg on the TV spots.

DO recalls a dream: "Clifford Irving telling me it was all his wife's idea."

Volkswagen Beetle becomes the most produced automobile in history, overtaking the Model T Ford.

Wed Feb 23

TFT meets with John Goodchild of Straight Arrow. "Book now off and becoming a reality." TV ads delayed until a week from Monday.

Nixon tours China. Great Wall. Forbidden City.

Thurs 2 March

TFT's twelfth and last show in the KPFK "Let's Eat" series. (Called "The Hilario Spacepipe Show," this one found Chicanos in Space, the President at the Wall of Mars, Yuri Yankoff singing "San Clamaron," and Charles, Walter and Eric trying to anchor the pieces together. THE MARTIAN SPACE PARTY was improv'd into life live; right there on the Last Radio Show in the last live series TFT would have until 2001. For some reason this show wasn't one of the 1972 syndicated series.)

Huge article by Mark Leviton on TFT for the UCLA *Daily Bruin* features our quote: "Our work isn't a metaphor for society, it's a metaphor for the universe."

S̲a̲t̲ ̲4̲ ̲M̲a̲r̲c̲h̲
DO edits 3 more "Let's Eat" shows for the syndicated series, which was later issued on ten half-hour reel-to-reel tapes.

Retired Deputy Director of the Bureau of Narcotics and Dangerous Drugs John Finlater joins NORML and reports that marijuana is less harmful to health than smoking cigarettes or drinking alcohol and eventually will be legalized. Around the same time, Dr. Bertram S. Brown, director of the National Institute of Mental Health, tells a news conference that marijuana should be decriminalized. Shortly after, a bill to make the possession of 5 oz or less of pot a misdemeanor is introduced in the California legislature by Assemblyman Alan Sieroty.

M̲o̲n̲ ̲6̲ ̲M̲a̲r̲c̲h̲
TFT tapes "only one" of the TV commercials for CBS. "Reports through the week excellent." Conferences with attorney RS on CBS contract, meeting at PA's.

DO sees college chum Richard Chamberlain in *Richard II*.

Ringo says the Beatles Fan Club will close at the end of the month. "We don't want to keep the Beatles myth going, since we are no longer together," he said in London.

T̲u̲e̲s̲ ̲7̲ ̲M̲a̲r̲c̲h̲
TFT continues mtg, works on new radio show for 3/30.

W̲e̲d̲ ̲8̲ ̲M̲a̲r̲c̲h̲
TFT continues work on the show, now known as THE MARTIAN SPACE PARTY, and on "the new album," and also designs Papoon Campaign. The Nat'l Surrealist Party is born.

DO sees *Wizard of Oz* and *42nd Street* on TV.

Thurs 9 March
TFT signs new 5-year contract with CBS. End of "exceptional week."

Sat 11 March
DO editing last two radio tapes. Goes to party for poet Ed Dorn.

Week of 13 March
"Three days of working on *The Martian Space Party* & associated projects. Last week in L.A. was one of the best times in our history."

Gov. Ronald Reagan says he has no plans to return to film acting and turns down role as Douglas MacArthur. Mrs. Reagan said she is opposed to legalizing marijuana.

DO sees *What's Up, Doc?*

NYC's Mayor John Lindsay said he would work for homosexual rights if elected President.

John Lennon says, "New York City is the center of the Earth," and plans to apply for permanent residence. Ringo is reported to be directing a film with Marc Bolan of T-Rex.

Wed 22 March
TFT "outlines remainder of the show."

Burt Reynolds poses for a nude centerfold in *Cosmopolitan*. A sidewalk star for Chaplin is oked by the L. A. City Council 11 to 3.

The National Commission of Marijuana and Drug Abuse recommends that private possession of marijuana for personal use no longer be a criminal offence.

Thurs 23 March
"Just about 2/3rds of the show finished."

Fri 24 March
TFT "works writing until 7 or so." DO meets with SG on the script.

Sat 25 March
TFT's commercial, featuring giant records and a car-dealer spiel, was shown, probably for the only time, on L.A.'s Channel 5.

Mon 27 March
DO throws the I Ching about *The Martian Space Party*. Duration changing to The Ting. "Restlessness as an enduring condition brings misfortune."

TFT meets at KPFK (the MSP performance is a benefit for the station) and has evening music rehearsal. Cyrus Faryar, producer of "How Can You Be," is music director and "the wives" are back-up singers. The broadcast has inspired a half-a-dozen songs for us to boogie down with.

At the time, CBS was advertising TFT as "The only rock group in the world that doesn't need music."

Tues 28 March
DO buys performance shirt with extra rhinestones at Turk's Western Wear.

TFT spends the day in rehearsal.

Wed 29 March
TFT rehearses "all afternoon and late into the night." The KPFK hall decorated as a Convention Hall by the volunteer Grassroots, led by Edgar Bullington.

Rolling Stone's review of *Dear Friends* comes out: "This album is us!"

The Christian Science Monitor says of Bozos, "This is the Firesign Theatre's *Finnegan's Wake*!"

"ANYTHYNGE YOU WANT TO!"
At the Martian Space Party
Photo by Dr. W. Deadjellie

Thurs 30 March
TFT has afternoon run-thru.

The MSP broadcast went on the radio live, and simultaneously on 16-track tape and 35-mm film, at 8:30 p.m.

"*The Martian Space Party* appeared to go off splendidly, with only minor things evident during the show. The audience — and there were lots of friends and people we hadn't been in contact with for a long time — appeared to love the entire experience."

Wed 5 April
TFT to studio to hear playback of MSP, recorded by CBS engineers out in a mobile bus. Continues discussion of next album.

THURS 6 APRIL
TFT meets at PA's to work on album — "sketching out ideas."

DO goes to Troubadour to see Harry Shearer in The Credibility Gap.

FRI 7 APRIL
TFT sees MSP film at screening room. There are more-or-less three camera angles covering the whole show.

MON APRIL 10
TFT works on film all day. "1st section pretty well done." Plan to finish editing Friday and shoot inserts the following Monday.

DO watches Chaplin on the very end of the Academy Awards. "So sentimental — made me cry."

DO reads entire galleys of *The Big Book of Plays* — "just excellent."

TUES APRIL 11
"Good long day in the studio — ended up at 10 with first two sections cut — viewed them — going to be a fine, funny film."

WED APRIL 12
"Very slow day but enough got done."

DO "totally distracted by The War on TV — shit!"

THURS APRIL 13
"Now we have a complete cut of the Convention."

FRI APRIL 14
"Worked all day but slowly."

Sen. Harold Hughes (D-Iowa) says he has smoked marijuana. "During World War II in Africa I smoked marijuana and it had absolutely no effect on me." He favors an amnesty for pot smokers in prison.

Sun April 16
   Set up miniatures on PA's porch for insert shots of Glutamoto attacking the Miniature Cardboard Village of Fudd until 3 PM, then shot until after dark.

Mon-Tues April 17-18
   TFT continues in editing room. "Endless dark hours."

Wed Apr 19
   TFT at the familiar CBS studios 9 a.m. to 9 p.m. "fixing up the track."

Thurs April 20
   "Very close to finishing" MSP movie. Screening for CBS and editing sound. Also, layout of photos for book almost completed.

   Lawrence Livermore scientists propose the existence of a giant planet beyond the orbit of Pluto which they call "Planet X."

Fri April 21
   DO spends a short day in editing. "Film was fine and to be finished up by PB & PP."

   "The men are on the moon!" (Apollo 16)

   (In retrospect, THE MARTIAN SPACE PARTY movie seizes the strong narrative count-down of Papoon's Nomination and the President's Blast-off, while revealing just enough of the side-trips to be tantalizing. It is a fine, funny film, even 24 years later.)

   TFT's 1970 "Electric Western," *Zachariah* showing with *Shaft* and *Celebration at Big Sur* this weekend in a triple-bill at the Airport Drive-In in Goleta.

Mon 1 May
   TFT begins working on a different concept for the next album, heavily influenced by the new material written for the MSP. "Started in writing page 1 — commercials which lead us on

into the 8-track."

Tues 2 May
"Developed very quickly the basic plot outline for "Not Insane." Worked quickly on plot development" Also, mtg with SG on film.

J. Edgar Hoover dies at 77. An 85-year-old FBI agent is, however, still on the job (as predicted by PP on *Dear Friends*).

Wed 3 May
TFT continues writing.

Thurs 4 May
Screening of MSP at CBS. "Spent afternoon continuing with "Not Insane," technical discussions, sounds, filling out the plot."

Mon 8 May
"Spent most of the day discussing movie with SG and dealing with business . . . the day ended with Nixon's Mining Hifong speech — so we all were a little blue."

Tues 9 May
TFT writes 6 more pages of NI. This includes first drafts of "Torment of Young Guy in Radio Prison" and "Mark Time & Crew Return from Planet X." The stories would intersect in a virtual world of merging media, watched over by WALTER — the supreme Watch and Listen to Everything Robot. "This is WALTER . . . "

The secretary of the 30th World Science Fiction Convention writes to inform us of "Bozos'" nomination for the 1971 Annual Science-Fiction Achievement Award (Best Dramatic Performance).

Wed 10 May-Thurs 11 May
"Not too much more work accomplished." (Rewrites of "Young Guy" and one new page of "Mark Time.")

Week's headlines: RICHARD NIXON REIGNS UNCHECKED. 'EXXON' NEW NAME FOR HUMBLE. PAINTING OF NIXON IN NUDE IS WITHDRAWN FROM ART SHOW.

Sat 14 May

DO's I Ching throw for *Not Insane, or "The Firesign Theatre vs. Dream Monsters from El Outer Space"* is Duration, changing to Limitation. "Thus the superior man creates number and measure, and examines the nature of virtue and correct conduct."

Mon 15 May

TFT spends six studio hours recording and building the 8-track collage which will represent "Radio Prison," an Earth-girdling sphere of ever-expanding transmissions, from vintage radio, foreign broadcasts and TV movies, to the noise of solar wind, all created from recycled ads, readings of Filipino comic books, gospel music, coverage of the Olympics in Tierra del Fuego and other bits from the "Let's Eat" radio shows.

"Came back to Motel — watched TV — the George Wallace shooting announced during our lunch."

"A good first day's work."

Tues 16 May

"Morning session went very well — boys playing music, so mood way up. Technical work very satisfying."

Wed 17 May

"Work progresses. By the end of the day we will have the base-tracks for the first 5 mins and music for the whole thing."

"Finished the back-tracks for 'Not Insane.' Very positive feelings all around. Good music and improvisation."

Sinatra comes out of retirement to croon at a fundraiser for VP Spiro Agnew, then vows it's his last public performance.

Sun 21 May
  DO's I Ching throw for "Not Insane (Continued)" is Coming to Meet, changing to Retreat. "There is a fish in the tank. No blame. Does not further guests."

Mon 22 May-Tues 23 May
  "The two days in the studio have contributed 7 mins assembled. Today, we ought to get into 'Young Guy' sequence."

"Got a mix this morning."

Wed 24 May
  "Finally got into recording 'Young Guy.'"

(This was TFT's sixth and last day of this final series of sessions working in the old CBS studios with engineers Bill Driml and Phil Cross. The results can be heard on the cuts "La Bomba Shelter" and "Young Guy, Motor Detective" on TFT's 1993 compilation *Shoes For Industry* on Columbia/Legacy.)

Tues 30 May
  DO "Proofed book pages (again)."

  DO's I Ching throw for "Keeping Not Insane" is Grace, changing to After Completion. "Grace in the hills and gardens. The roll of silk is megre and small. Humiliation, but in the end good fortune."

  A man named Laszlo Toth smashes Michelangelo's "Pieta" with a hammer.

Wed 31 May
  TFT decides to discard portions of work already written and recorded.

Thurs 1 June
  Photo session at PA's for "Not Insane" album cover — burlesque of a Japanese Monster movie poster, probably "Rubbergon Dumn Toyko."

FIREMAIL/THE MINDLESS FELLOWSHIP — TFT's first "official" fan club starts up in Lincoln, Nebraska.

Fri 2 June
TFT writes two pages of a new scene in which Young Guy, his girlfriend Miki and his butler Rotonoto listen to The Lizard on the pirate radio, then SG arrives ("Somebody must be downstairs, Boss!") for mtg which ends abruptly and TFT goes home.

Sat 10 June
TFT decides on no further meetings at this time. Phone calls continue throughout June.

News reports: Hoover leaves his half-million dollar estate to his friend Clyde A. Tolson. According to Gallup, President Nixon's popularity is at the highest point — 61% approval — in nearly two years, after his Summit meeting in Moscow. Roper's survey finds that 51% of American adults believed they would obey, if, as soldiers in Vietnam, they were ordered to shoot all inhabitants of a village suspected of aiding the enemy. Elvis, 37, is appearing at Madison Square Garden. *The Goon Show* reunites for a photo op with the Duke of Edinburgh and other Royals. Marijuana penalty reduction defeated on the California Senate floor. The Dog-Face Butterfly approved in the State Assembly as California's State Insect.

Wed 28 June
DO's I Ching throw for "tomorrow" is Opposition, changing to The Creative. "One sees the wagon dragged back, the oxen halted, a man's hair and nose cut off. Not a good beginning, but a good end. The companion bites his way through the wrappings. If one goes to him, how could it be a mistake?"

Thurs 29 June
Screening of MSP movie on the big screen at the Director's Guild theatre in Hollywood. TFT all present, along with

"Grassroots" campooners, friends and show-biz types. "The showing was enjoyed."

EPILOGUE

THE MARTIAN SPACE PARTY played all over the country in the fall of 1972 and became a Science-Fiction Underground Classic. Mention was made in *The New Yorker* of the Nat'l Surrealist Party and Papoon's "Not Insane!" slogan. John Lennon was photographed wearing a "Not Insane!" button the following April.

TFT's album titled "Not Insane" was released in the late fall to confused reviews. Finished during the summer, it was finally a collage of the new studio recordings, parts of the MSP performance, and our old favorite, "The Count of Monty Cristo," recorded on tour in 1970. The contemplated storyline and newly written but un-recorded scenes were never used.

A year came and went. Proctor & Bergman teamed up for *TV or Not TV* (in which two guys try to produce everything for a homemade cable station by themselves while media pirates surf on their sine waves). I produced "How Time Flys" with Steve Gillmor, in which Mark Time does return, in the year 2000, alone and forgotten, from Planet X, and has his hologram records of the trip stolen by an unscrupulous entertainment entrepreneur. Austin began work on *Roller Maidens from Outer Space*, a Surrealist Detective Story with Music, which takes place out on the thin boundaries between electrons, where the Apocalypse is always in progress.

Fit the two hours-plus of these three albums together with "Not Insane" and the "Let's Eat!" shows into a single time-and-space condominium and you'll have 1972's long-awaited "next Firesign album."

Easier yet, join us in person on that Historic Night, March 30, 1972, at THE MARTIAN SPACE PARTY!

Oh yes, TFT didn't formally meet again until late August 1973, to begin work on "The Giant Rat of Sumatra." The Golden Age had become the Sober Seventies. Not Insane!

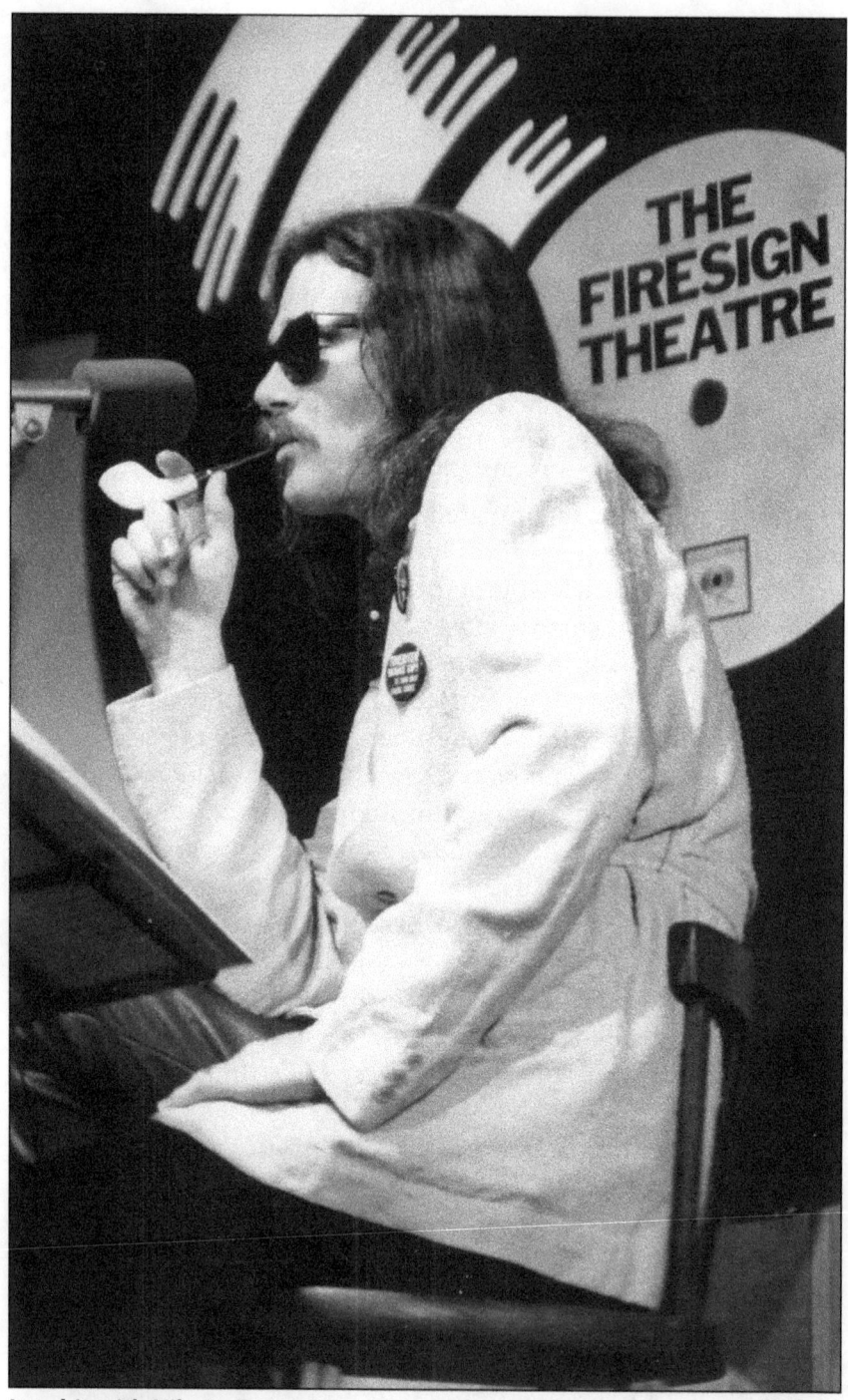
In orbit with Hilerio Spacepipe

12. "IF THIS ISN'T ESCAPE, WHAT IS?"

Sure, we survived. Let's skip Forward into the Past. The stories of "The Giant Rat of Sumatra," "Everything You Know is Wrong" and the rest of the 1970s remain in my crystal balls. We were together again in 1980 and working on radio, writing a movie and a play and a new album — so why not do something easy, like a musical? A CD liner note. (1993)

FIGHTING CLOWNS
The Firesign Theatre's Full-Frontal Musical Review
"Odd how heavy the tensions are. The 80s — what a bomb!"
DO's Diary, 26 January 1980

What you are about to hear is a recruiting show for the Reagan Era. Three big acts on the Center Stage — America's Favorite Love Boat People — The Eight Shoes! Supply Side Balladeers — The 101st Fighting Clowns! And — Just Say No! to Fuddz! Hostages, hot tubs, freedom fighters and nuclear war! Free! Only the interest on a trillion dollars!

This album got going in mid-January 1980 when TFT made a date to play The Roxy, a handsome Sunset Strip rock club, on the coming Leap Year weekend. We'd been in the big glitter box a couple of times before, with new comedy reviews — "The Owl and Octopus Show," "The Joey Demographico Show," but this loomed as a unique opportunity to strut our newest stuff to a new decade. It also loomed very soon.

We were covering the 1980 election campaign for NPR's "Morning Edition," and we would continue to argue about politics and policy among ourselves while we did so for months to come. We were writing song parodies profiling many of the hopefuls in the presidential field, contemplating post-modern biographies of Carter and Reagan, and testing alternative candidates like Vice President George L. Tirebiter and Phil Austin's implacable ex-movie star, Daffy Duck.

We were also arguing among ourselves about what direction The Firesign Theatre itself should take for the Eighties. We had a national radio outlet in an election year. People were talking to us about starring in a TV show. We were all interested in getting into the movies without buying a ticket. Taking the Roxy gig made us focus on preparing a show that might really show us off. As the show took on an identity it became a musical revue.

For the next four or five weeks we were together three or four days at a time, writing sketches about the invasion of Afghanistan and America's come-on with the Soviets. A Brechtian rant appeared (we had recently appeared in a Brecht piece, with music by Hindemith, playing violent clowns, live in Ojai), then Phil A's reggae named "Bill," and finally the Eighties Generation juicing up on 245TTCDDDESDDTCE. There was a lot of war talk in the news and folks were hotly partisan. Our show would be dressed in Cold War colors — Dead Black & Hot White.

February 11 marked 100 days in captivity for the hostages in Iran. We wrote them in too — into a piece we called "The Towel Play," because towels figured as costumes in each of the blackout sketches. The blindfolded bureaucrats joined singing sailors-on-leave from several WWII musicals, punk wannabes from the Valley Mall, and coke-snorting Hollywood hot-tubbers in commenting on the confrontational times.

After a day or two of smoggy spring, it rained. It rained day after day in mid-month and work mud-slid to a halt. The Phils' houses flooded. I tried to drive Peter home one afternoon. We drove — or dove — to the axle-deep bottom of Deep Canyon, where we got turned back by a neo-mythic road-crew, looming out of the tropical twilight mists, a truly lifesaving Spielberg moment.

Reaching high ground in the Valley for that night, we were introduced to a TRS-80 and an "interactive" game to play on it. It was spiffier than video games, and video games had outstripped pinball for pizzazz. The pixilated options of the Pentagon's ultra-simulated war-games were already heat-seeking trigger-happy young consumers, and now we could adventure in cyberspace. These notions landed first in the opening number of "Fighting Clowns," and a year later in "The Pink Hotel Burns Down," a ten-minute demo for some high-concept entertainment software.

We were still writing on a second vaudeville sketch called

"Meanwhile in Billville" (about the Olympics, I think) when band rehearsals (led by the excellent Richard Parker) began at The Roxy on February 25. The next day an album deal mushroomed — we'd record all six Roxy performances 24-track and make an LP from them! Zowie! The performances went very well, especially "Leap Year Saturday." (Those are real audience reactions you hear, natch.) Double zowie! By the following weekend, it seemed we were going to have a movie deal too, at MGM. Triple zowie, but in negotiation.

❖❖❖

By mid-month March we were spending weekends at Cherokee with Fred Jones, sweetening takes from the Roxy, laying in new music tracks (Jeff Baxter's blazing guitar riffs, and the brass section) and writing, improvising and recording new material. "Did the Hot Tub scene — 3 hours writing and 3 minutes recording," I wrote in my diary. We were still arguing about the Future, and it wasn't hard to wind ourselves up for the Fuddz scene, in which we fight, briefly, about breaking up the group. "The Carter Song" (chronicling the never-to-be Liberal Democratic Succession) vanished from the concept (to be issued much later as a "picture-disc" single).

Yet nothing seemed to hold a Firesign album together as the finished pieces accumulated until the last day in the studio, when we improvised the short wraparound scenes in which an audience of Us Clowns is hustled into the Big Show. "Something very simple and introductory," I wrote. "This album seems almost to be a segue from Bozos."

As Election Year dragged on, the first recording contract vanished, leaving the album to be issued in November on "Firesign/Rhino." We wrote our "How Can You Be?" adaptation of Homer's *Odyssey* only to be scuttled (along with Metro's minimoguls of the moment) on the studio's way to ruin. We even ate lunch with Julia Phillips, pitched the *Airplane!* guys, got a new manager, new agents. By November we were writing another show for the Roxy and preparing a national tour — among the last things we would do together for the rest of the Teflon decade.

❖❖❖

"Fighting Clowns" captures the "full-frontal" on-stage performances of February 1980, the in-studio improvisations of March, and the belligerent, self-satisfied mood of the Empty

Eighties still to come. For the 1981 tour, we interpolated the following scene into "The Eight Shoes Present the American Pageant." Read it first. It'll help make Reality less painful!

PETER: So long, Gramma. I got my orders from the government — collect — and I only have ten minutes to leave town.

DAVID: It's going to be dangerous, Sonny.

PETER: Only the food, Gramma.

DAVID: What's this badge on your uniform, Sonny?

PETER: That's the 101st Fighting Clowns emblem. See him smile? And it says our motto — "Semper Humorous" — Always a Laff!

DAVID: What are they gonna do with ya, Sonny?

PETER: Well, they drop us at night, without a parachute, holding on to a humongous big watermelon. It confuses the enemy radar into thinking we're 500-lb bombs.

DAVID: Oh, oh! Better leave me a picture, Bucky — you're not gonna be back for a long time!

PHIL A: And he wasn't!

PHIL P: 'Cause after they dropped him on Dunquerque, they dusted him off . . .

DAVID: And dropped him on Düsseldorf. And then they dumped him out over Dresden

PHIL A: And doped him up and dove him into the D.M.Z.!

SONG [to the tune of "Sweet Betsy from Pike"]:
   Oh, let's paint a tear
   For the brave Fighting Clowns —
   Pushed out of the airplane
   They fall to the ground.
   Their arms round their melons
   They salute us with pride
   Their shoes all inflated
   They fell down and died!

Tirebiter's Triumphant Return
PHOTO BY PATRICIA PENCE

13. BACK FROM THE SHADOWS
The Firesign Theatre's 25th Anniversary Reunion Tour

Another CD liner note. Briefly turned up again, like four or five bad pennies, we were not working as the Firesign after two basically unhappy tours. It seemed as if this CD set might be our final testament. The show had been created to preserve the legacy of the early albums and the recording demonstrated the journey our characters had taken. (1994)

About a year ago — April 1993 — my wife Judith caught me after another ten o'clock dinner-for-eight to say, "Look, I've got a houseful of comedians on my hands, and it *isn't* funny!"

At that point, Phil Proctor was sleeping on the futon in the living room after staying up to all hours trying testily to enter the day's adlibs and script changes into my middle-aged Mac. Peter, Patricia, little Lilly and their several suitcases were stashed in the guest room. Preston, at seven months, was acting like a baby (who could blame him?), and Orson, soon to see his father live-on-stage for the first time, was coming down with the flu. I myself was on dubious prescription drugs to keep from losing my voice.

We were in our last week of rehearsals for what was billed on the Paramount Theatre marquee in downtown Seattle as the Firesign's "25th Reunion." Reunion it was. We had last performed together in 1981, appearing in various moldy basement rathskellers, leftover Disco boites, and college "halls," fully equipped with two spotlights. Our wonderful, stoned, bozo-nosed fans were out there, a few of them, but mostly The Firesign Theatre was up against the Empty Eighties.

Now, dearly beloved, the Eighties was the Decade of the Nasty Comic, MTV, and Ollie North. The Evil Emperors begat the New World Ordure. Shit happened. Firesign fans, pushed out of the cradle into the post-Kissenrockafordafeller era, made up their minds to do the Right Thing — put aside the bong and the beard and Get On With It. Prophesy took a back seat to profits.

By 1993, a few of you had made a million or so by stringing ones and zeros together. A whole lot more were working in recording studios, radio stations, major newspapers and fabulously popular TV shows. You were, as we were shortly to discover, everywhere! Some of you were even women and kids!

Our one night stand at the Paramount was a sold-out smash. The audience greeted us as long-lost friends. We were back. You were back. We had no place to go but on the road.

These CDs are as permanent a record of mutual affection as can be digitally managed. As Phil Austin (who, fortunately for all of us, was then staying at his own island home, some 50 miles south as the eagle flies) said to me during rehearsal, "What year is this?"

Somehow, the quarter-century of ups and downs mellowed with laughter into a show that headlined our favorite characters and our fans' favorite lines. Nick and George and Rocky and Mudhead gathered themselves out of the shadows and reminded us why we had clung together in the first place. The folks out there in the shadows — you folks — reminded us we had done it for them — for you.

So here we all are, having a swell time in suburban Philly, newly Clintonian D. C. and laid-back Berkeley. Have yourself a houseful of comedians. We promise not to stay for dinner.

AN AFTERWORD
FROM GEORGE L. TIREBITER

Back in the Sixties, when I first met the Firesign boys, I was living in a tie-die teepee hidden deep under the Indian tobacco trees, in the hills behind Universal City. I was flattered that they were amused by a few of my stories of the glory days of Tinseltown, and even more so when they involved me, or someone like me, in a new comedy record.

In their present Reunion Show, they have straightened out the kinky narrative which preserved their surrealist reputation on disk, and give the audience a straightforward, if abbreviated, account of my retirement from the Hollywood Madhouse. Missing are a few details — my blacklisting, perpetrated by my ex-wife, "Bottles," and the tragic auction in which so many moviegoers' memories were sold to the lowest of bidders.

To answer a frequently asked question, no, I do not die and go to heaven at the end. In fact, these ingenious chaps restored to me my Youth, lost so long before when it was necessary for me to pretend to be professionally elderly in order to disguise my tender years.

My fling with the Nat'l Surrealist Party in the Seventies, my reemergence as a Radio Revivalist in the Eighties, my present happy, and genuine old age today, are due to the affection and support of four or five of the craziest guys the Antic Muse hath ever inspired. That they have reassembled, if even for a short time, does them great credit. When the time comes to present them with their justly deserved golden doorstops for Lifetime Achievement, I hope to be there to hand them out, myself.

4 or 5 Crazee Guys

THE WORK
"Forty years of Firesign Theatre collaboration."

Over a period of forty years, the members of The Firesign Theatre have accomplished, together, in various combinations and separately, a large body of work in all of the entertainment media. For those readers whose Fun with Firesign ended in the early 1970s, let the following be a reminder of the body of work released and published under our "brand." The Stage and Radio categories are only partial.

AUDIO

Waiting For the Electrician or Someone Like Him (1968)
How Can You Be in Two Places at Once When You're Not Anywhere at All/Nick Danger, Third Eye (1969)
Forward Into the Past/Station Break (1969)
Don't Crush That Dwarf, Hand Me the Pliers (1970)
I Think We're All Bozos on This Bus (1971)
Dear Friends (1972)
Not Insane! (1973)
The Giant Rat of Sumatra (1973)
Everything You Know Is Wrong (1974)
In the Next World, You're on Your Own (1975)
Just Folks — A Firesign Chat (1977)
Nick Danger and The Case of the Missing Shoe (1979)
Fighting Clowns (1980)
Shakespeare's Lost Comedy (1982)
Lawyer's Hospital (1982)
The Three Faces of Al (1984)
Eat or Be Eaten (1985)
Back From the Shadows (1994)
The Pink Hotel Burns Down (1996)
Give Me Immortality or Give Me Death (1998)
Boom Dot Bust (1999)
The Bride of Firesign (2001)
Radio Now Live (2001)
Papoon For President (2002)
All Things Firesign (2003)
Box of Danger (2008)

RADIO

Radio Free Oz From the Magic Mushroom (KRLA, 1967)
The Firesign Theatre's Radio Hour Hour (KPPC, 1969)
Dear Friends (KPFK, 1970)
Let's Eat! (KPFK, 1971)
Anythynge You Want To (NPR, 1979)
Campaign Chronicles (NPR, 1980)
Fools in Space (XM, 2001-2002)
Firesign on All Things Considered (NPR, 2002-2003)
Firesign Live in London (BBC4, 2005)

STAGE

The Martian Space Party (1972)
Anytown USA (1974)
The Owl and Octopus Show (1979)
Joey's House (1979)
Meanwhile in Billville (1980)
Fighting Clowns (1981)
The Firesign Theatre's 25th Anniversary Show (1993)
Radio Now Live (1999)
Radio's a Heartbreak (2005)

FILM & VIDEO

Zachariah (1970)
The Martian Space Party (1972)
Everything You Know Is Wrong (1975)
The Odyssey (screenplay, 1980)
Weirdly Cool (2001)

PUBLICATIONS

The Firesign Theatre's Big Book of Plays (1972)
The Firesign Theatre's Big Mystery Joke Book (1974)
The Firesign Theatre's Fun Page (1975)
The Firesign Theatre's Campoon '76 (1976)
The Apocalypse Papers (1976)
Bozobook (1981)

"I'M BEN BLAND"
A Commercial Interlude

"Hello there and such a happy day to you again today. And it is the All-Day Matinee and I'm Ben Bland, here every day with another great film, *The Whispering Greek*, with Farfel Knabe and Rochelle Ragout. A chance to win a hundred unmarked bills for life tax-free on the Matinee's Sort-Out-The-Stars Contest. And familiar words from the good people that keep this image of me on your screen day-after-day. People like Woody Torquemada . . ."

WOODY: Woody Torquemada for Zepmaster School of Flying. I'm taking a minute to talk to Eddy Catalina, a Zepmaster's recent graduate and already in a good job aboard a petroleum sky-train. Eddy, what was the training? Was it what you had expected?"

EDDY: Better. I go crazy in classrooms, so all the docking and loading practice made it easy to take. That simulated 8-hour cross-country flight, shoot! After that you really feel what it's like to pilot a big Zep!

WOODY: Wait 'til you go up — fully loaded! — The only way to fly. Pilots earn 50 to 100 double-bucks a year, so why not you? Call Zepmaster now. Get the fact-filled booklet on your new career in the air — from mini-blimps to hunkin' big dirigibles. Call Zepmaster now at the number on your screen . . .

". . . and I can assure you they can help you get a job. They're the biggest — with a new Zep school for you disaster relief victims at Valleymart Plaza. You know, there's a brand-new Imperial Householder Policy that virtually maximizes your minimum protection while excluding wear-and-tear, marring, scratching, deterioration, inherent vice, latent defect, mechanical breakdown and everyday rust and mold, not to mention taking care of additional living expenses if not caused by earthquake, volcanic eruption, landslide or mudflow, except for your storm doors. And I guess that's important. For you folks living within a hundred-mile radium of Devil's Canyon Liquid Nuclear Gas Plant, remember — NO policy can insure you against loss by atomic reaction, radiation or contamination, controlled or uncontrolled. Call your Imperial Man today — he has the right form for your personal liability."

OLLIE: Hi! I'm Ollie Oxenfree and Gibberson's does it again! You ladies said you wanted a bigger selection in the Meat Department and we've got all-time low prices on fresh whole-bodied USDA Grade A fresh-boiled great-horned owls. Just great for entertaining! Check any other big chain's advertised price claims on chained owls and we won't just change 'em — we'll make sure it never happens again! Because of this exciting offer, we must limit two owls per family. Remember — over ten-thousand of your neighbors are driven mad every week by the prices at Gibberson's!

NEIGHBORS: *"Gib-Gib-Gibberson's where
The shop-shop-shopping
is fun-fun-fun!"*

"Wow, owls! I'm Ben Bland and it's ethnic cleansing all this week on Ben's Internet Graveyard Matinee. I'm always here and if your serotonin level is as low as mine, I know you'll have nothing else to listen to while you do your Geriatric Studies Homework.

"Matinee's brought to you this morning by *GATES OF HELL* brand-new walled and gated maximum security community out there in the Bosky Hills of Prozaktown, New Jersey. Surrounded by protected County Reforestation Reserve and vast tracts of smog-free Saudi-owned golf

lands and grazing greens — How safe is it?
Easy — they won't give you a key! And if
you think you can't afford it, join the folks
who already live there — they can't afford
to sell!

"It's *GATES OF HELL*, a hopeless timeshare — or
a Timeless Homestead — at The Village.
You'll sing-sing the prisons — praises — of
these condo-like lifestyle entertainment
units, where you program the perfect vacancy
options for you and your legal companion.
OK . . .

"Now, all the advice you need to start working
again in the Twenty-First Century, from the
good folks Out There in orbit — at Western
Colonial Technologies! . . ."

MONTANA WOMAN: I used to be a lumberjack,
before the trees were small. Now, I'm a
Space Colonial . . .

RUSSIAN GUY: I used to hustle used fuel rods —
now I hustle Passive Mass Catchers . . .

JERSEY GIRL: I really wanted to go someplace
ELSE! That why I decided to try for Powersat
Programmer

STRAIGHT GUY: I used to work borders for the
Feds . . .

ALL FOUR: Now we work for the Colony!

WEIGHTLESS PITCHMAN: Change YOUR life! Call
now! Follow your Specific Impulse into High
Orbit, with help from Western Colonial

Technologies. Yes, the Colony is now a fact — you can watch it growing ever-larger up in the sky tonight! YOUR career can grow with it! Western Colonial Technologies! 87 percent of WCT grads are in Outer Space right NOW! Why not YOU? Press 1-800-L5 and talk to one of our career advisors on line — they're weightless too!

"That's 1-800 L5 or you can e-mail directly to me, Ben Bland, at my webspace. Say, if you're watching me now, you might need this reminder . . ."

BUPCO MAN: You can do it! Build your own Power Plant — start today! The same jerks who call you a 'nut' now are going to be standing in line to reap the rewards after the bottom falls out! Beat zoning restrictions! Cover all bets! Feel 'Family-Safe' in your own home! This week, learn to build a 'paper-clip' computer, backyard pyrolosis furnace to make fuel-oil and charcoal briquettes, or even a safe, portable atomic device, using declassified documents and materials easily available at all BupCo's, Creditline and Repair City Stores!

"I don't know why, but that commercial reminds me of a funny story about this movie, 'Psycho on Gunstreet 13.' It seems that after guest corpse Faye Dunnaway was done away with by the sharp-tongued wit and Howard Hughes fingernails of little Freddy the Cabbage Patch zombie — her husband — played by that bad guy from 'Cheers' before he was famous — Ded Manson — was supposed to grieve over her torn and bleeding body, but there they were, all in makeup and special effects and everything and Manson turns to the director and says — 'I can't cry' and the director says, 'Think of something terrible that really happened to you, hunch your shoulders over and heave.' So he does — later he said he was thinking about this dog of his that got run over — and he starts to weep, and the cameras roll and he's sobbing and suddenly Faye — sorry, it's Cloris Leachman, that's right, anyway, she suddenly gags and sits up and runs off the set screaming: 'He's got green snot coming out of his nose!' And sure enough, it's in a famous outtakes reel they won't even show on 'America's Funniest Hard Copy' he's crying so hard goo is running out of his nose!

"Catch that scene coming up tomorrow on Ben Bland's Mystery Sci-Fi Rippoff Theatre's Brainscan Matinee screening of 'Psycho in Gradeschool, The Sequel: Eat It Raw!'

"We'll be back . . ."

"And that's good advice. Here's some more from Ben — Have you been watching your neighbors and friends leaving the Metroplex in ever-increasing numbers? Ever wished YOU could leave behind the high costs of imported water and minimum pollution requirements? Yes, you CAN, in an ecologically-improved setting along Big Rio River, where there's no high buildings, no telephone solicitation and no high-intensity ethnic incursions.

"That's the name of it — *DOMARAMA SHORES* — where space-colonization technology preserves a natural wilderness of controlled fishing and boating adventure experiences. Believe Ben Bland — living here is actually living!

"You've just got to get more information about it, because once you spend a long weekend under the Dome, near a luxurious home-site YOU can afford, you won't want a chance to get away. Call collect. Think of it! Fishing for giant catfish, a secret golf-course, even fifty consecutive car-washes free! Just press this number now . . ."

"While we're waiting for this technical interruption, let's take a look at the Job Bank, thanks to the State Department of Life Situations Service Center. In the Smogtown area, a position for olive reamer trainee. Salary plus lottery credits. This job has a high moisture content, with energy retrieval and pit disposal. You must be over 18 and bondable. Two hundred clams a week.

"In Metroplex South, here's a Computer Bar Operator. Must be well qualified in Bubble and Busbar Programming. Separate lines, gravity-operated, no cross-mixing and happy hour prices all day. Salary and housing negotiable.

"Let the State help you improve your present life situation. Visit the office in your area and ask for specific information on these and literally more job advantages. It's a service of your Government. Now, the rest of this great movie, *The Whispering Greek* with Madge Twerly and Edgar Burlington."

"This is Ben Bland with Metroplex News Bleeds at 1:20. High Court says handicapped children could be bussed twice to achieve balanced integration. Asian Airlines passengers struck by ozone amnesia over Pole. Free hairdos for homeless mothers reduce child-abusing tendencies. And more on that big Laundry Protest with Matsuo Martinez and Yolanda Watanabe on Junk News at 6 and 11."

"You know, if you have loved ones *YOU* love — even yourself — who need help now — and I'm proof, because I used to be one of them — act in time!

"It's Basic Skills Smoking, Reading and Driving Clinics, where — yes, even YOU can learn to get out of your house even if you haven't been able to in years. Locations to help you in near-by Rural Park, Woodland Farms Mall and on South Appian Way in Condo Marina. If you can't help what you're doing to yourself, learn how — at Basic Skills, where there's no pain and no programming — we promise!

"The movie's over, so call right now — that number's on your screen. One of Basic's trained therapists will answer you in person — NO impersonal tapes!

"This is Ben. From the Matinee, good-bye until the same time, again . . ."

STATION ANNOUNCER: It's a jellyfish illusion when Jerry impersonates a 1949 Hudson tonight on *Celebrity Standoff*!"

PART TWO

Dr. Elmo Firesign, O.D.

Tirebiter for Veep!

THE SAGA OF CAMPOON '76

PROLOGUE FORMER HOLLYWOOD STAR TURNS POLITICO . . . 77

OCTOBER 1975 PAPOON LAUNCHES BALLOON! . . . 78

JANUARY 1976 EXCLUSIVE MEDALLION OFFER! . . . 80

MARCH 1976 TIREBITER — GRASSROOTS FAVORITE — ANNOUNCES CANDIDACY . . . 82

APRIL 1976 AMERICAN HISTORICAL SILVER SLUGS! . . . 85

JUNE 1976 TIREBITER TESTIMONIAL TURNS THE TIDE . . . 87

JULY 1976 BISON-TENNIAL SLOW GUN CONTEST! . . . 89

JULY 1976 FIRST BISON-TENNIAL CONVENTION . . . 91

AUGUST 1976 SHOOT FOR THE MOON WITH TIREBITER & PAPOON! . . . 91

AUGUST 1976 TIREBITER UPDATE . . . 93

SEPTEMBER 1976 TIREBITER ON POT! . . . 95

SEPTEMBER 1976 NARCOLEPTIC THREAT? . . . 96

SEPTEMBER 1976 THE RICHARD M. NIXON STORY . . . 97

OCTOBER 1976 TIREBITER SCANDAL DEEPENS! . . . 98

OCTOBER 1976 CAMPOON SUSPENDED! . . . 100

NOVEMBER 1976 JUNTO EN SURREALISMO! . . . 101

NOVEMBER 1976 PAPOON WINS AGAIN! . . . 101

EPILOGUE IT REALLY HAPPENED! . . . 103

There is no one to blame.

PAPOON
FOR PRESIDENT

(You know he's "Not Insane!")

FORMER HOLLYWOOD STAR TURNS POLITICO
Prologue

George Tirebiter, radio star and director of wartime musical films, retired to a quiet life as a novelist and occasional script doctor, supported by a series of science-fiction stories and an undercover relationship as a spy for Howard Hughes. As the mid-1960s rolled along, Tirebiter returned to radio as a weekly commentator for the little-known Nat'l Surrealist Party. He moved from his longtime bungalow in Los Angeles to suburban Glendale and ran for City Council on the NSP ticket in 1966.

When the NSP held its first presidential nominating convention in 1971, Tirebiter worked tirelessly behind the scenes for candidate George G. Papoon, to whom he was distantly related. The campaign (or "Campoon") introduced the slogan "Not Insane!" into political discourse. Tirebiter made political capital with the youth movement by "turning out, tuning on and dropping in," and, in fact, by deciding to live in an Indian teepee where he welcomed such visitors as Tiny Doctor Tim, the Clown Squad and The Firesign Theatre. He even drove a hand-painted VW Bug from Jack Poet.

With the collapse of the Nixon regime and temporary residency of Jerry Ford, the Campoon of 1976 loomed as a do-or-die effort for the Surrealists. Tirebiter, who had regained sudden public notoriety when he was threatened with violence while announcing the Best Picture Award at the 1975 Oscars, sought support from the Firesign, but the group was divided. The dada half of the team supported another masked candidate, known only as "The Electrician," while the surreal contingent saw the over-riding necessity to establish a "Not Insane!" government in the Bicentennial Year.

George Papoon announced his candidacy in October 1975. Tirebiter hit the trail shortly after and, at the summertime "Bison-tennial" NSP conventions, won the Party's support. It was an exciting, exhausting year and one that would change Tirebiter's life. Here is that saga, as reported in the pages of *Crawdaddy Magazine*.

PAPOON LAUNCHES BALLOON
October 1975

George G. Papoon, responding to encouragement from all parts of These United Snakes, announced his candidacy for U. S. President last week from his home in Wentzville, Missouri.

Papoon, who was standard-bearer for the Natural Surrealist Party in the 1972 campaign, continued to claim that he was the real winner in that disputed "election."

"Despite Senator Eagleton's copy-cat claims to be Not Insane, no McGovernment ever had a chance," Papoon reportedly stated. "Why, there are folks out there who haven't been represented since 1938!"

Cocoons for Papoon are being organized in many neighborhoods, in an effort to get the N.S.P on the ballot in all 52 states. According to N.S.P. Provisional Co-Chaircreature Dr. Elmo Firesign, discussions are underway for a "Bison-tennial Convention" in 1976 at which Papoon will officially be placed into nomination, along with the convention's vice presidential selection.

"This nation urgently needs a display of real Grassroots Surrealism," proclaimed candidate Papoon. "If I am not elected, I *will* serve. If I *am* elected, I will not serve long."

EXCLUSIVE MEDALLION OFFER!
The Ten Events That Swamped America
January 1976

The Nat'l Surrealist Party is pleased to offer, exclusively and for profit, a new series of valuable "turtle-neck medallions" from the famous Buysometennial Mint. Each medallion has one of the TEN EVENTS stamped into .999 fine pot metal on one side and a shiny reproduction of Salvador Dali's "Happy Face Watch" on the reverse. Wear them on a chain, hide them or throw them away! A Bison-tennial offer you won't want to resist!

Here are the TEN NOSTALGIC EVENTS you will be getting D.O.A. as chosen by the editors of *Peep Hole Magazine*:

7. Destruction of the Last Buffalo (1873)
8. Discovery of the Hamburger (1900)
9. Regular TV broadcasting begins (1928)
10. The Marijuana Tax Act (1937)
11. The First Singing Commercial (1939)
12. The Los Angeles Freeway Plan (1940)
13. The First Credit Card (1950)
14. The Playboy Philosophy (1958)
15. First Photo of the Whole Earth (1967)
16. The MGM Auction (1970)

Send anything of value, along with your name and number to:

BIG MEDALLION OFFER (actual size 3/4")
P.O. Box 4306
Channel City, CA 93103

TIREBITER — GRASSROOTS FAVORITE — ANNOUNCES CANDIDACY
March 1976

We stopped downstairs after a Sootte Salade lunch in the Museum of Modern Art the other day to view "Babes in Khaki" (1942), the first in an introspective series of films by the former "boy genius," George LeRoy Tirebiter. The movie looked a bit dated, but we could easily see how a jaded, war-torn Hollywood could have been revived by Tirebiter's daring surrealism and unconscious musical numbers.

An overflowing crowd of well-dressed young people stayed after the film to applaud the genial, long-haired Tirebiter, attired comfortably in a raw silk smoking jacket, red-crested ascot and gray plaid trousers of an old-fashioned cut. He recalled several amusing moments in his career and then made a startling announcement, which brought the audience to its feet, cheering and chanting "Not Insane!"

"Ladies and gentlemen," Tirebiter said, "I take pleasure today in confirming rumors which have lately surfaced in the *Times*, *Post* and *Barb*. I will be a candidate for Vice President on the Nat'l Surrealist Party ticket."

Later, we met Tirebiter in his lavish hotel suite, where he explained to us that Grassroots pressure had made him announce his candidacy.

"That, and my realization that only an aging pro like me could challenge that other old fart in a race like this!"

We asked him if his recent public appearances around the country in "Radio Laffs of 1940" had changed his life.

"I should say so," he replied, lighting the omnipresent cigar and crossing his slippered feet on the coffee table. "I'd been retired for several years, you know, before getting involved with a fling at Japanese showbiz. Pretty soon, though, I started thinking of myself as a has-been again. Besides, I could never learn the language. So I sold my partnership and moved out to the California desert. When my agent said I ought to go on the road again, I told him nobody cared about the Golden Age. Thank God I was wrong!"

We enquired if he could fill us in on the mysterious rumors

surrounding his childhood, some of which had him as an illegitimate foundling.

"I'm grateful for the chance to clear this thing up," he laughed. "I was born in Chicago on December 7, 1920. I never knew my real father, but Mother told me he was a great English gentleman and that I was their love-child. I have deduced," he winked at us, "that the Old Man was none other than the notorious detective of that time, Hemlock Stones. Of course, he had been an actor in his youth, so naturally I was predisposed toward the stage."

"Will your being born out of wedlock have any effect on the electorate?" we asked rudely.

"I think the public *wants* a bastard in office," he remarked cheerfully. "We've had so many of them. But at least I'm an honest bastard!"

Tirebiter's challengers in the race to be George Papoon's running mate include the wasp Axarfncvxxl; a German Shepherd named Henry Quixote, reported to "do a heavy Bogart imitation"; Delbert Dindledorc of Baltimore, who turns into a police horse when tired; and the young political activist, movie star and jailbird Kim Kool. We asked George how he felt about the opposition.

"I've met Ms. Kool," he replied frostily. "We had a bit of a confrontation at last year's Academy Awards, if you'll remember. She recently called to apologize for trying to kill me and I told her I was glad she was out on probation. Of course, we're both Surrealists, but I belong to the Radical Conservative wing, while she remains a dedicated Independent Anarchist. I trust we'll have ample opportunity to debate our differences in the Future. As for the insect and those crypto-animals, Mr. Papoon has assured us that his co-candidate will be chosen by popular vote at the upcoming convention. I believe I have a better chance than these other creatures, largely because of the Nostalgia Craze."

Tirebiter's "little honey" of the moment — an attractive chorus girl named Cindy Lou Saltenstall — reminded him of pressing business in the next room and George kindly showed us the door.

"See you on the Funway, sir" we said and took the elevator to our office.

AMERICAN HISTORICAL SILVER SLUGS!

A Buysometennial Mint Hit

The Nat'l Surrealist Party slyly offers a limited edition of famous American bullets, authentically copied in 9.9% virgin silver-toned metal. You'll long collect and treasure these bits of Our Cherished Past because each month we'll ship to you such sentimental mementoes as:

> The Efficient Revolutionary Roundball
> Civil War Mickey and Mini Balls
> Colt .45 pop-nose Equalizer
> Manlicher-Carcano 3-in-one Slug
> and
> A genuine Election Night Special with actual simulated cyanide jacket

Each life-size casting comes in a fine bronze-styled casket with descriptive headstone. Also available in sensational Duck Metal — never needs polishing!

Just tip us off to your location, how much you have to spend, and general anxiety level. Then stand back, because your first Historical Bullet will be fired off to you FAST!

Write: BIG BANG OFFER
% The Buysometennial Mint
P.O. Box 4306
Channel City, CA 93103

Tirebiter on The Stump

TIREBITER TESTIMONIAL TURNS THE TIDE
June 1976

Former radio and film star George LeRoy Tirebiter has advanced to a commanding lead in the race for Surrealist Veep, as a result of heavy California Campooning. Tirebiter, whose well-preserved and familiar features continue to delight audiences everywhere, has proved that political experience is no asset in today's electoral process.

With his feature films and other non-political appearances banned from the television by the Unequal Time Rule, Tirebiter has continued to use the stage and radio to bring his charismatic charm and Radical Conservatism to audiences from Duckburg to Channel City.

Recently, Southern California Surrealist Delegates and Volunteers threw a testimonial sack-lunch for Tirebiter in world-famous Earthquake Park, a peaceful oasis in the Tri-City Area which had once been a three-level underground freeway exchange and motel intercourse near Oil Beach.

Supporters from such animal and vegetable groups as Dogs United For a Good Time, Friends of Grass and Trees, A.N.T.S. International, the Famous Insects League, and Beets and Carrots Underground were in attendance, as well as representative humans speaking (as only they can) in opposition to the Program of Insane Solutions offered by Demopublican politicians.

Tirebiter himself, looking tired but energetic, spoke for ten minutes on the general subject of "Surrealism in Your Daily Life," and once again made the major points with which he has been identified during his Campoon to date — direct taxpayer participation in the allocation of the Budget Pie (The Anton Chekoff Voluntary Taxation System); the proposed Federal Job Shuffle (a random re-employment of all public employees whose skills, such as "espionage agent," "army general," "economist" or "tax collector," are out-moded and unnecessary, in healthy outdoor activities where they can do little harm); the E. R. P. Amendment, which extends equal rights to native-born American plants; and the total elimination of Federal subsidies to or contractual arrangements with corporations "whose products or services do not contribute to peace, the conservative use of appropriate energy sources, the development of truly useful and inexpensive consumer items and the preservation and renewal of the biosphere."

A surprise appearance by Nat'l Surrealist candidate George Papoon late in the program was taken by those present to constitute an endorsement of Tirebiter for Veep, even though Papoon made no such formal statement.

"I will accept the creature chosen by my party's convention," Papoon said. "However, Mr. Tirebiter is well qualified for the position and promises to stay on the West Coast in order to bring balance to the Federal Government."

The cry of "Let George George and George do it!" rang out across Earthquake Park and most of the human members of the crowd put the sacks they had left from lunch over their heads and joined together in a traditional Dragon Dance, symbolizing the beginning of both the New Year and the Good Old Days.

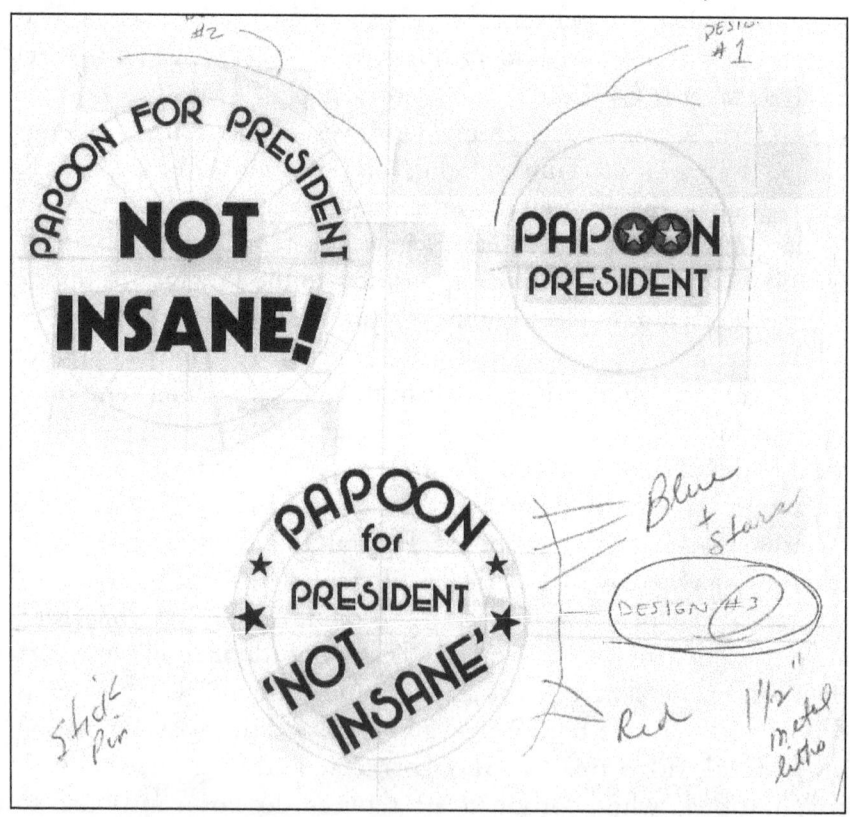

BISON-TENNIAL SLOGAN CONTEST!

Sponsored in Part by Nat'l Surrealists

Here's big news about that Big Bison-tennial Slogan Contest they've been having! After receiving over 200 suggested national slogans from housewives, kindergarten kids and the terminally unemployed, the final choices have been narrowed down by a secret committee of former CIA directors.

PICK ONE!

1. USA — The Freeway's Way!
2. Stuck Fast, Stuck American!
3. Forget the Past — And Don't Worry About the Future!
4. America! Just Like on TV!
5. Not Insane!

Remember — you get to vote on these slogans and the most popular phrase will be awarded an appropriate statuette on stage at the Hollywood Palladium by either an over-exposed television star or a Las Vegas call-girl. Or both!

Send Your Choice To:
Slow Gun
Box 38 Special
Smithandwesson, NJ 007

A Job What Needs a Man For a Man What Needs a Job!

FIRST BISON-TENNIAL CONVENTION
As reported in the Santa Barbara News-Press

A rally, the "Shoes for Industry Revue" and a flashlight parade will be public highlights of the first Bison-tennial Natural Surrealist Party and Convention to be held in Santa Barbara July 31 and August 1.

The party, whose favorite son, George Papoon, is running for president of the United States, said it plans a series of workshops on campaign appearances, district organization and other matters.

Santa Barbara, referred to as "The Big Avocado" by David Ossman, local Papoon supporter, was chosen for the convention because "every place was full" in Los Angeles, he said.

Convention events to be open to the public, Ossman said, are the "Shoes for Industry Revue," set for 8 p.m. July 31 at La Casa de la Raza; a flashlight parade immediately following; a rally at 12:30 p.m. August 1 at the Acacia Restaurant in Isla Vista; and a live broadcast of the convention over KTYD radio at 8 p.m. August 1. The broadcast, he said, will be open to the public and will be aired from La Casa de la Raza.

The revue, Ossman said, will feature "The George Papoon Story," "Moon Men from Detroit" and "Everything You Know Is Wrong."

SHOOT FOR THE MOON WITH TIREBITER & PAPOON!
August 1976

George G. Papoon proudly accepted his party's nomination as Pre-Residential Candy-date at this month's Surrealist Convention, held in Channel City, California. As his "running mate" the Convention endorsed George L. Tirebiter, whose tireless activity in putting the bite on the part set him far ahead of the various other candidates, animal and vegetable.

In his acceptance speech, Papoon hailed NSP Party workers in these words: "Fellow Surrealists, whatever you are! And, whatever you are, I am *you*! Because you demand a voice of Not Insanity to speak your views on the madness of the present system!

"Because the Demopublicans want to put the Carter before the Voter and give you the You-all and the U-Haul! And because the Repocrats want to replace the Bozo with the Has-Been and the Oil Man with the Milk Man!

"If you continue to speak for me the way you have, the result will be even more Surreal! Remember — the Surrealism of Power is not Responsible — it's Electrical! But the power of Surrealism is not Electoral — it's something to laugh at!"

Tirebiter, hastily written acceptance speech in hand, was warmly greeted by the members of the Convention, notwithstanding some intense rivalries for the "Veep" spot on the NSP ticket.

"Dear friends," Tirebiter said, "I am running for the Vice Presidency in 1976 because I wanted to do something original for my country's Bison-tennial, and because I have reached the age when I'm tired of paying for things that no one really wants, with money that no one really makes.

"With your support, George Papoon and I will triumph over the Atom-Powered Monster, who even now lurches toward San Clamaron, eager to be reborn!"

Finally, in a brilliant display of Natural Surrealism, George Papoon demonstrated that he was whatever anyone wanted him to be, by existing only as an Idea in their minds and hearts. Tirebiter, showing a well-developed taste for the corporeal, quickly left town with the Idea of Papoon, remarking, "So much for time and space! We're going to take a week off, go fishing, and think about it."

TIREBITER UPDATE
August 1976

RUNNING HARD: Vice-presidential candidate George Tirebiter put on his red track shoes for reporters recently and expressed his enthusiasm for the ripple-soles. "They give me good traction," he said, "and a sense of speed and movement, even when I'm sitting down, which I'm going to do now."

A TIP O' THE HAT: Asked by a group of supermarket bag-boys why he did not affect the traditional surrealist brown-paper sack worn by his running-mate, Tirebiter pointed to his decorated plastic boater with a smile. "I'm simply bringing balance to the ticket. No one knows just who Papoon is under the bag. Everyone knows who's under this hat, because it has my name on it!"

SLOGAN: George Tirebiter approved his Official Campoon Slogan at a casual ceremony held in the Gold Room of Joe's Café. Final choice was "A job what needs a man, for a man what needs a job!"

"FRINGE BENEFITS": Noting recent sex-scandals in Froggy Bottom, G. L. Tirebiter promised that there would be "no hanky-panky at the public's expense" in his executive office. "I will personally pay for all my own hanky-panky," he added.

HIGH TIMES: Accused of being "nothing but a good-time Charlie" by Demopublican Party Hack Charles Goodtime, Veep Candidate Tirebiter admitted he liked drinking, smoking and carousing in moderation, but added, "I avoid the real killers — white-sugar-fear and raw-meat-hate."

ACTING CAREER: "After we are elected, I plan to resume my professional career," stated candidate Tirebiter. "I think that having the Vice President appear in a few good movies will do wonders for the National Image."

DEBATE CHALLENGE: George L. Tirebiter has challenged the

other official Veep Candidates to a public debate. "One of them is a conscious agent of the Bavarian Illuminati," Tirebiter claimed, "and the other is an obvious loser. Our problem is only to find out which is which."

TIREBITER ON POT!
September 1976

It is well known that George Papoon and George Tirebiter have both been longtime supporters of total repeal of Federal legislation concerning *cannabis*.

They have, however, recently come out in favor of the proposed Marijuana Amnesty Act, which would restore all civil rights to persons convicted of violation of the Marijuana Tax Act of 1937, provide a Personal Presidential Apology and present a $1,000 cash award to each victim of the "War Against the Flowers." (Costs of the cash award will be taken from the CIA Opium Slush Fund.)

Papoon also recognizes that "legalization" of trade in *cannabis* would quickly result in the monopolization of the market by melty-national corporations. This would eliminate thousands of small-time connections and cause gross economic hardship. Papoon and Tirebiter have therefore also endorsed the Home-Grown Act of 1976, which provides that anyone may grow *cannabis* on land that is his to cultivate. This act also places a heavy tax on finished "joints," to discourage a large industry from springing up.

Tirebiter has recently admitted to smoking "pot" himself. "It would have been Insane not to experiment with the stuff when I first came upon it. Having tried it, it would have been Insane to discourage its use. Personally, I enjoyed the temporary feeling of 'being a criminal,' because normally I am quite law-abiding and never drunk-drive."

NARCOLEPTIC THREAT?
September 1976

Rumors have it that George Papoon suffered a sudden and lengthy recurrence of his notorious narcolepsy upon hearing the news that his running-mate, George "The Fox" Tirebiter, had been involved in a sex-scandal. Sources close to the candidate admitted that he "fell asleep a bit early" several nights last month, but that this in no way indicated a relapse of the mysterious illness which causes him compulsively to fall asleep at the "darndest times," as one staffer put it.

Tirebiter himself, awakened from a nap at his recent Blue Moss Motel press conference, would make no comment about his own recent tendency to nod off while thinking about his troubles.

"I can't even spell the damn thing," he spluttered. "Nor can I spell yarborough, hagiology or sauerbrauten — not to mention panjandrum!"

"I thought I told you not to mention that," whispered Tirebiter advisor George Antrobus, to which the candidate began to reply, but fell promptly to sleep, sighing softly, with a contented smile on his untroubled face.

THE RICHARD M. NIXON STORY!
An Exclusive Screening for Surrealists

Only once in a generation comes a story so timeless — so packed with laughs and thrills — so rich with tears and jeers — so filled with the beloved characters you've read about in *Readers Digest* and seen on TV. A film so big, so honest, it could only have been made in today's People's Republic of China!

THE RICHARD M. NIXON STORY!

From his uneasy childhood, through his odyssey of personal crisis, to the triumph of his international diplomacy, this motion picture will stand tall as the most truly American epic of your lifetime!

> "Magnificently neurotic! Visibly balding!" says Pauline Kael of Jack Nicholson's towering performance as The President.
>
> "Never was Washington brought so faithfully to the widescreen," says TIME. "Hal Holbrook makes an unexpected J.F.K. and Chuck Connors will win plenty of votes for his athletic portrait of Lyndon Johnson."
>
> TODAY says, "You'll like Ike again and again, as sensitively played by Gene Hackman."
>
> PEOPLE says, "Cloris Leachman is frightenly good as Pat."

With an outstanding supporting cadre from the August 9th Revolutionary Film Collective and Special Guest Star Frank Sinatra as Mao Tse Tung!

THE RICHARD M. NIXON STORY!

A Red Star-Rebozo Production, rated G — Gosh! Expletives Deleted! It's a movie you'll want your kids to remember, too!

TIREBITER SCANDAL DEEPENS!
October 1976

In the wake of last month's sensational revelations, Vice Presidential candidate George L. Tirebiter's place on the Nat'l Surrealist ticket seems either more, or, possibly, less secure.

The fresh-faced Cindy Lou Saltenstall, Tirebiter's "little honey," whose recollections of her year-long "adventure" with the candidate touched off an endless series of intimate disclosures, has recently left the Coast for parts unknown, taking with her the manuscript of her book about Tirebiter (tentatively titled "Who IS That Man?") "for further revisions," as she put it.

"He may be a lover, but he sure isn't no dancer," Miss Saltenstall said demurely before she boarded a Beets/Air East flight in the company of her friend Candy Clock.

Answering questions at a hastily called press conference in the Blue Mouse Motel in Heater, California (close to his desert home), Tirebiter (who was forced by these events to make a clean breast of his private life) appealed to the voters for understanding.

"I'm afraid that I've always been a bit naïve where women are concerned," Tirebiter confided. "But I do like to have them around me! I've tried most of the Hollywood vices and women seem the most stimulating of them all. I certainly would not want to face four years as Vice President," he winked, "without female company, though I hardly think I'd have to put them on the payroll!"

Asked if he was upset with Ms. Saltenstall's plans for a book on their affair, Tirebiter shook his head.

"No, not a bit. Although I am interested in reading it, especially if it's as titillating as I've heard. You know, at my age, compliments come in few forms, most of them literary."

Around the country, some citizens' groups were organizing against the Papoon-Tirebiter ticket, citing health and morality as their two major issues. Surrealist supporters of the candidates feel the need to deemphasize such matters and concentrate on Papoon's popular "Not Insane" policy promises, but at this time it is not known whether the spreading scandal will erase Papoon's early lead and bury the Campoon in its final two months.

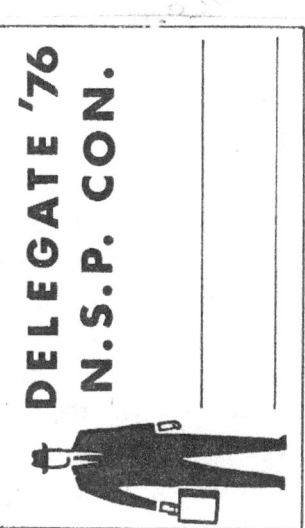

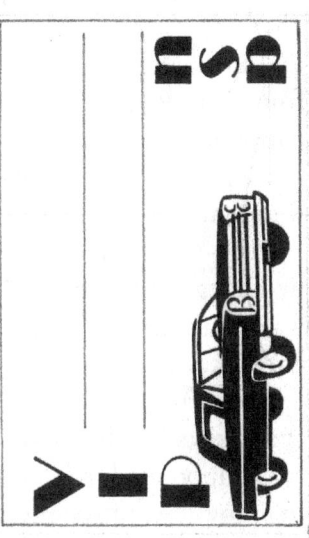

CAMPOON SUSPENDED!
October 1976

Natural Surrealist Party Co-Chaircreature Dr. Elmo Firesign has announced from Party Headquarters in Channel City, California, that active Campooning by the Papoon/Tirebiter ticket will be suspended for the weeks remaining before Election Day.

"We have decided to rely on an informed electorate," Dr. Firesign said. "This last-minute hustle for votes is undignified. Besides, what more can be said to an intelligent human than to proclaim his Not Insanity at the polls in November?"

Firesign explained that volunteers were already in the fields counting the wild animal vote as birds and beasts of all kinds come close to small towns (and certain "safe" cities) in order to be counted. Domestic animals have been barking, purring and whinnying their approval ever since the Dog Days of Summer. Migratory creatures have been stopping off at such polling places as Animal, Missouri and Butterfly Haven, Florida, to have their noses and tails counted for Papoon and Tirebiter.

"It's not too early to tell," the Doctor explained. "The conclusion is foregone. It's all over but the cheering. Oh, we understand that the other candidates in the race will tell us they've won — but you know that's Insane! They never win and we always lose!"

Candidate George Papoon, who was reported to be suffering from a mild case of the shuffles after months of wearing brown paper bags, retired as usual to the complete privacy of his home in Wentzville, where he plans to stay during the next four years of his Residency.

Veep-nearly-elect George Tirebiter, caught with his flaps down by Exaggerator reporter Joe Beets at the Hollywood Airport on his way to an undisclosed destination for a well-publicized rendezvous with a certain "little honey," mumbled something about "too much damn hard work," and was heard to say, "sometimes I wonder if he even exists," as he boarded his flight.

Campoon volunteers across the nation welcomed this opportunity to enjoy the fall weather, watch football and look forward to a new era of inter-species co-operation.

"By the end of this Bison-tennial Year," noted Dr. Firesign, "I believe we may be able to tell at last if there is any Future for Comedy in Peacetime. If there is, Papoon and Tirebiter will continue to serve their country in 1977!"

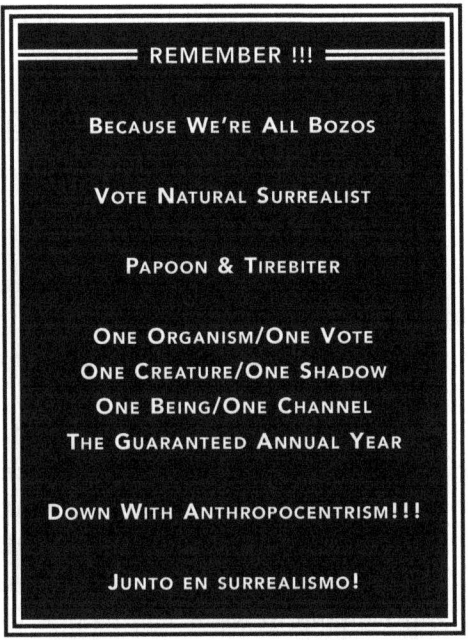

PAPOON WINS AGAIN!
November 1976

Humans, creatures, maxi- and micro-organisms all over these United Snakes once again let it be known that they had their own and one another's best interests in mind at the polls earlier this month, as they flew, ran and slithered in support of George G. Papoon.

Many unidentified two-legged voters wore paper bags on their heads and cast ballots for themselves. Dogs everywhere howled for Papoon, joining a chorus of wolves in a show of militant solidarity.

"We've smelled him, and we know he's one of us," barked Dr. Porter T. Pupp of the Grand Old Dogs Society, interviewed on his way to a dinner and rock-toss.

A rare performance of the Whales-Play was given in the Humboldt Current Auditorium, way up north, providing sufficient energy to enlighten most of the West Coast, south to the Orange County line.

Elsewhere (actually Elsewhere, Mississippi), a sudden show of force by Killer Bees for Connelrockakissafordadoleafeller was beaten back by Brave Bats, formerly counted for Papoon opponent Count Tranquilla, but now squarely in Papoon's camp.

In a statement issued from his Wentzville home, George Papoon acknowledged his victory, saying: "Dear Friends, once again Natural Surrealism has triumphed over both National Realism and Regional Nastyism! Once again, enough of you have run right along with me to win the Human, not to mention the Universal Race. To Papoonatics in loyal Cocoons all over this great land of 'Rs,' my gratitude knows no boundaries! Now, I would like to take my sack off and sleep for a while, leaving the rest of the changes up to you."

So saying, he stepped inside his charming home and shut the door firmly behind him. Meanwhile, Vice President-elect George LeRoy Tirebiter celebrated with a costume party at the Raymond Chandler Hotel in the little desert community of Hollywood.

"I needed this job, you know," he said to an interviewer from *Peep Hole Magazine*, "and I intend to work very hard at it — whatever it is — from now on. Yes, for the next four guaranteed annual years, Americans will be able to keep laughing at politics, knowing that Tirebiter is but a heart-throb away from The 'Residency!"

EPILOGUE

Strange, even surreal as it seems, all of that actually happened. Over the course of a year-plus, I shepherded a national theatrical event which included nearly a hundred active "Cocoons for Papoon" in 23 states and the District of Columbia. There was even a second exhausting party convention, in September in Topeka, Kansas. A Topeka publication called "The Toiler" kept a detailed record of Campoon events and *Crawdaddy's* monthly columns brought forth the story you've just read. There were, in addition, films, art work, a lot of writing and collaborative ideas exchanged with friends all over the country. An inauguration ceremony was held in "Channel City" early in 1977.

George Tirebiter was reborn in the process. The Firesign Theatre, which had disintegrated into Proctor & Bergman, and for a while, Austin & Ossman, stayed alive as the background identity behind Campoon '76. The notion and inspiration of our collaboration was released into the atmosphere, where it was wholeheartedly picked up by fans who continued to elaborate on the nine Columbia LPs we had released to date.

Thirty years later, I consider the Campoon to be one of the most complex and rewarding collaborations of my so-called career. I had, in fact, celebrated the Bicentennial by running for (Vice) President. It took more energy and skill than I had ever before put into an improvisation. I discovered, above all, that if I said I was running for office, no matter how weirdly, people took me at my word. It was and is The American Way. (2006)

The Price of Fame
Photo by Carter Blackmar

Part Three

General Otis Starsucker

The Roots of Poon

SIX TALES FROM THE UNTOLD HISTORY OF THE US

As told to George L. Tirebiter by George G. Papoon,
With an Introduction by Mr. Tirebiter
And Genealogical Notes by Philo Gemstone, O. D.

1. INTRODUCTION ... 109
   BY GEORGE TIREBITER

2. MY LIFE, BRIEFLY ... 110
   BY GEORGE G. PAPOON

3. FILLMORE POON, ... 113
   OR, THE FIRST PRESIDENT TO
   SLEEP THROUGH HIS TERM OF OFFICE

4. POLLYANNA VAN POON, ... 116
   OR HOW GEORGE WASHINGTON
   MET HIS VALLEY FORGE

5. JEAN LE POON, ... 120
   OR, PIRATE-PATRIOT OF NEW ORLEANS

6. TOPEKA POON, ... 124
   OR, THE MAN WHO INVENTED ALL-AMERICAN CHEESE

7. MAJOR ZEPADIAH POON, ... 127
   OR MOUNTAIN MAN TRICKED BLIND BY INJUNS

8. DUDLEY POON, ... 130
   OR, FIRST SHAKESPEARIAN ACTOR TO TOUR AMERICA

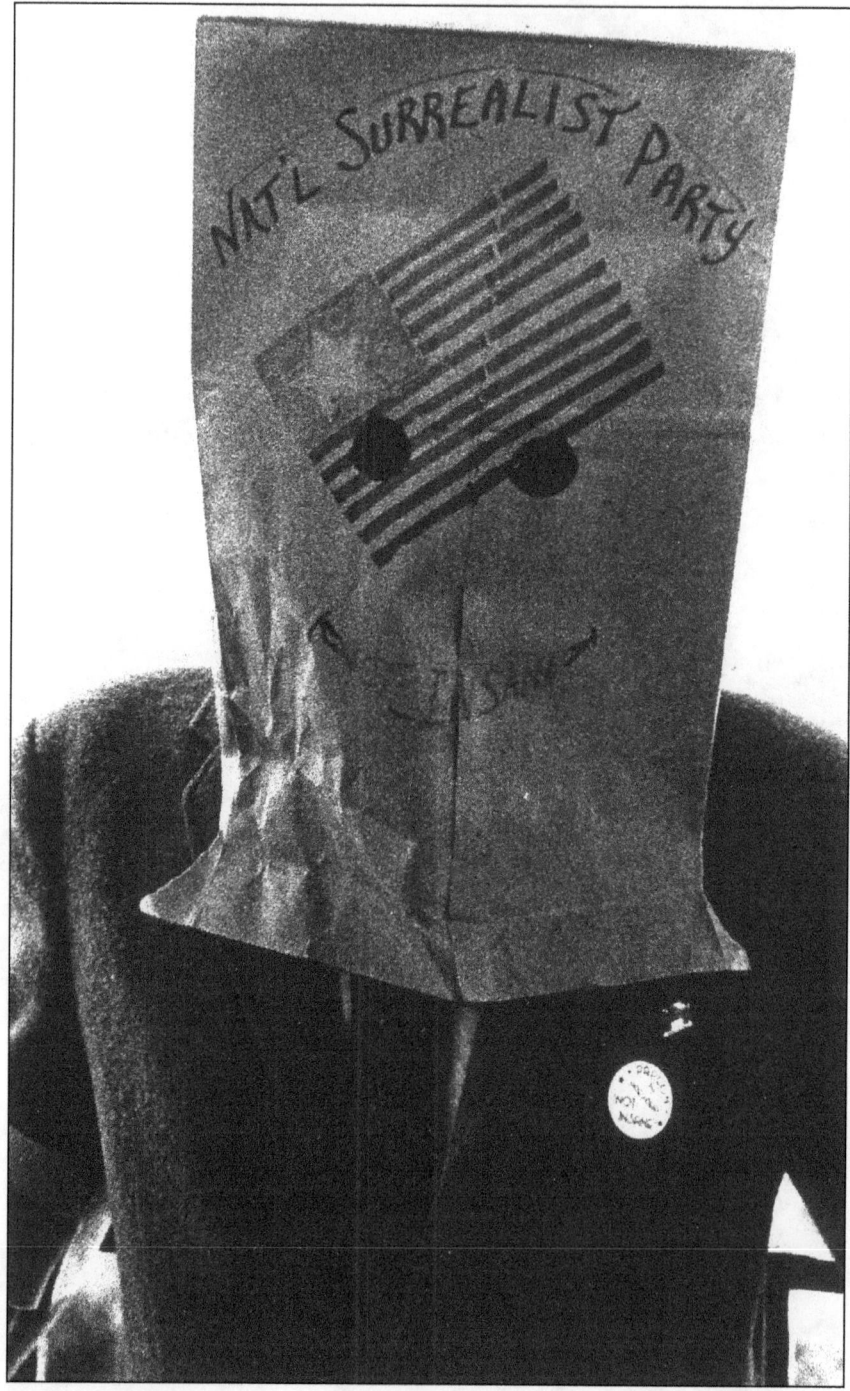

George G. Papoon

INTRODUCTION

One of the signal pleasures resulting from my strenuous campaign for the Nat'l Surrealist Party nomination for Vice President was to have the opportunity to meet and become close friends with the man whose paper-bag disguise concealed him from all but his immediate family and most trusted advisors.

Since the 'Resident (as many of us like to call him) and I spent uncounted hours together in old autos and grounded airplanes while on the Campoon Trail, he had ample opportunity to lose his accustomed Middle-Western reserve and regale me with stories of himself as a youth and of his many ancestors, whose lives were so amazingly intertwined among the roots of American history.

In the months which passed after our election to high office by the freely enfranchised biosphere, George Papoon returned to his home in Wentzville, Missouri, from whence he offered frequent "Not Insane" solutions to some of the more interesting problems confronting Americans during those post-War Seventies.

I, however, have engaged myself in collecting a number of George's tales, some of them having seen publication during the Campoon, others never before told. The 'Resident has himself carefully perused my manuscript and caught many errors of omission, adding many degrees of detail to his original off-the-cuff telling.

In addition, I have had the professional services of Dr. Philo Gemstone of Solid State University.com trace back the Papoon (or Poon) family tree. His notes are appended to the text.

I take pleasure in beginning with 'Resident Papoon's own biography which he dictated to Dr. Elmo Firesign in a phone call early in the race. I hope you will enjoy these memoirs and through them gain insight into the man we recognize as our leader. I remain, radiophonically yours,
GEORGE TIREBITER

MY LIFE, BRIEFLY
By 'Resident George G. Papoon

I was born in 1913[1] in Poonton, Kansas, which was then much closer to the Panhandle Indian Reservation than it is now. My father, George Sr.,[2] was a plains farmer of sturdy English stock[3] — a kindly man who understood the changes of nature and the habits of animals better than the ways of city people.

My mother, Mamie Cox Papoon,[4] was both a suffragette and a good cook. Between caring for her family and attending meetings at the Precilla Hall, she was always busy and wouldn't have it any other way. She and my father were distantly related and had a great-grandfather in common — the infamous Andy Gump,[5] known during the Civil War as the "out-house king."

My brother Dave[6] and I grew up in the cheerful community of Poonton, which was not unlike the small towns we used to see portrayed in movies made on Hollywood back lots. Dave and I graduated from high school a few years apart, blessed with a similar bent for machinery and love of open spaces.

---

[1] October 31, 1913 is presumed to be GGP's actual birthday. The Poon County Birth Register shows November 1, but this appears to be a result of negligence by County Clerk Heber "Bud" Hawkins.

[2] GGP, Sr. (1864-1955). Born in Poon County, Kansas, lived in Poonton most of his life, died in Ballew Memorial Hospital, Topeka.

[3] GGP traces his family back to Phillip Lord Poon (1608-1669), the only son of the noted actor-explorer Sir Dudley Poon and his Native American bride, Princess Little Laughter of the Hohosmokit Band. After his parents sailed back West and no more was heard of them, Phillip settled down at his Welsh estate and sired Phillip Lord Poon (1639-1690). Estate and title passed on to Chester I (1670-1742) and then to "Crazy" Chester II (1701-1800).

[4] Mamie Cox was the daugher of wheat farmer Andy Cox and banker's daughter Francis Gump. Born in St. Louis in 1867, she passed away in Wentzville in 1948.

[5] Andy Gump registered several U. S. Patents between 1861 and 1870, among them the popular spring-operated Crescent Moon design. He spent several years in jail for war profiteering after the Union Outhouse scandal during Grant's administration. His name has become synonymous with detached facilities. His son Chester became a wealthy St. Louis banker. Daughter Hanna escaped an oppressive home life to pioneer on the prairie.

[6] David Belasco Papoon was born in Poonton August 8, 1917 and stayed on the family farm until he was drafted in 1941. He served with the much-decorated K-9 Armored Division during its distinguished service in France and Germany. After the war, he joined the Small Animal Administration, retiring in 1975 from his position as Deputy Undersecretary for Supply and Reinforcement. He lived in Sunny Fraud, Arizona until his death in 1998.

I took up with some friends who worked odd jobs at Lincoln Airfield and by 1935 I was flying the U.S. Air Mails over Arizona and Nevada, where there was open space aplenty. So much, in fact, that I soon left the desert run to older men and joined "Ace Cochran's Air Aces," a literally fly-by-night carnival team. We barnstormed across the Midwest in search of adventure, gas money and girls who looked like Jean Arthur.[7]

I must have still been searching when I joined the Navy in 1938, hoping to pilot a zeppelin in the Dirigible Corps.

The heat was turned up high in Europe in those days and after a year of duty in Pensacola I was tapped for Naval Intelligence. Then came the war, an eventful period filled with opportunities for me to serve some of our most powerful leaders as a member of the Liaison Command and Diplomatic Relations Study Group. My happiest moments were spent as advisor on Sumatran affairs to the Commander-in-Chief at the Yalta Conference.

After the War, I entered Columbia University to study Law on the G. I. Plan. New York was an exciting place in those years and I pursued an interest in the art and archeology of South-Eastern Asia while preparing for an otherwise uncertain future.

During this period, I was contacted by a few old friends who offered me occasional assignments for the new Central Intelligence Agency. I decided to become a full-time agent in 1951 and was posted to Goonrat, Sumatra, where my "cover" job was to be librarian at the local U.S.I.A.

Of course, I actually was the Bureau Chief, but my appointment was so secret no one was authorized to look in my file, which was sealed and never opened. Naturally, I received no orders and the only spying I undertook was a brief investigation of a certain Indonesian noodle which I had mistakenly assumed to be an escaped Nazi war criminal. My superiors back at the Company assumed that their man in Goonrat was doing what he was supposed to do and so I did very little for nearly ten years.

It was a lazy, almost idyllic life in a beautifully under-developed country. The most memorable events of the time were my marriage

---

[7] Jean Arthur was then appearing in "Tri-Motor," an air-circus saga also starring Clark Tracy (Monotone 1937).

to Eleanor T'Ang,[8] the First Lady of my Heart, followed in a couple of years by the birth of my son, George III.[9]

I spent a great deal of time in an archeological dig near the ruined temple of Ampere Wat, then in danger of total destruction by the rebels as a result of the local Rattan Wars. It was in these steamy environs, deep in the bamboo forests, that I first stumbled across the true meaning of the Summer Rat Dance. It was this startling discovery and its hideous aftermath that finally resulted in my early retirement. I was invalided home with severe recurring shuffles and intermittent narcolepsy.

Eleanor, little George and I returned to a small home once owned by my grandparents in Wentzville, Missouri, where I attempted to recover from what we hoped would be a temporary mental confusion. Fortunately, my government pension gave me enough to open "Poon's Farm," an old-fashioned Indonesian noodle house, located in a recently abandoned bank building on Blumhoff Street.

Many of my childhood friends said that this seemed an unusual course for my "already exotic" life to take, but that didn't matter, given the electric fevers that frequently overtook me. I celebrated my fiftieth birthday with an outdoor curry barbeque, traditional Buddhist street dance and a sudden, dimly-remembered trip to Bismark, North Dakota, where I awoke from what my doctors called "overload narcosis."

It was not until 1969 that I was able to regain contact with the outside world, thanks in large part to the elimination of my shuffles by Dr. Bernard Beanbag, the television psychologist. It was he who gave me my Certificate of Not Insanity.

Hearing of their search for a 'Residential candidate who was truly "Not Insane," I sought out the leaders of the Nat'l Surrealist Party in 1972 and offered them my candidacy. Our platform of total enfranchisement has won for me the highest office in the land, the capstone to a life of public service.

---

[8] Eleanor T'Ang gives her birthdate as June 1, 1930. Her mother, Carlotta van den Moon, was the daughter of a Dutch East Indian bureaucrat and his "guttenfrau." Her father was a Sino-Sumatran tour guide who ran safaris to Ampere Wat, Skull Island and the Jamocha Coast in the years before the Japanese occupation. She and GGP were married in Goonrat, Sumatra in 1953.

[9] George III, born April 1, 1955, has always been known as "Jack." He attended Clown School in Hard Notch, Kentucky, and still lives in the "little White House" in Wentzville.

THE SAGA OF FILLMORE POON

George told me this story early on in our race for the 'Residency, after a fine, home-cooked supper at his modest Wentzville home. "I'm not the first of my tribe to serve as 'Resident," he observed to me over a rum-punch. "My ancestors were as hardy and foolish a bunch of Americans as ever walked across the country. My Daddy knew all about 'em. Handed the stories down to me." I settled back before the fire to listen as my running-mate closed his eyes, folded his hands across his belt-buckle and started to reminisce . . . (GLT)

There are many odd stories told about political Poons (*George began*), but maybe the strangest of any of my Daddy's forebears was Fillmore Poon — Senator Fillmore Poon[10] of Kansas. His rise and fall were sudden and his exile profound. Believe it or not, Fillmore was the unlucky thirteenth President of these United Snakes!

Now, as a boy, I had never heard Fillmore's name mentioned at the Papoon or Gump[11] family reunions, where nearly everybody of consequence was toasted sometime over the long weekend with strong blackberry wine. It wasn't until a trip to Washington during the Second World War that I finally heard of the affair that had all but purged the Senator from the very (*George winked broadly*) purgeable pages of the Congressional Record.

I was then a young Naval officer, assigned as liaison and aide to the now nearly translucent Henry Hoppendorf — as you know, one of FDR's "inner five" and a man whom some said owned the man

---

[10] Fillmore Poon was a grandson of Zepediah Poon, one of the so-called "Five Poon Boys of Kentucky" who were all married at one time or another to Nancy Noop who was GGP's great-grandmother.

[11] GGP's grandmother was Hanna Gump (1825-1885) who was a daughter of Andy Gump. His mother Mamie was also related to Andy Gump, who is thus GGP's great-great-grandfather on both sides of the family. Mamie's cousin Marmaduke Gump was the famous founder of the country-music dynasty The Gump Family and Japanese Pop Hero of the Seventies, Hideo Gump (Star of "Radio Prison") is GGP's cousin three times removed. Humorously enough, George Tirebiter himself was once married to a cousin of Hideo Gump's.

who owned the bank that held the mortgage on the whole USA.

I remember, it was one chilly, dismal Washington winter morning. Hoppendorf and I were riding together in the Senate Underground on the way to a routine meeting of the War Club, when the old gentleman idly spoke my name.

"Papoon, George Jr., eh? Damn funny dog tag, Lieutenant."

"Yes, sir," I said. "Used to be just Poon, sir, but my Grandaddy William James[12] got it changed on him, 'cause they always called him 'Pa' Poon."

"Huh!" snorted Hoppindorf and peered at me over his pince-nez. "Poon, is it? I don't suppose you know," he continued, lowering his voice, "that for one dark moment in our nation's history a single Poon held America's fate between his slippery palms?"

"I surely don't, sir," I replied.

He then recalled to me how Fillmore K. Poon (my cousin several times removed) had grown up in the badlands of Bald Knob, Kansas, seen a wicked youth and joined the repressive Corn County Regulators in '39. He then rose slowly through state political ranks and was appointed Ward Heeler by the Governor's private secretary in gratitude for fixing a by-election in '44.

"Some said he'd sold his soul to get where he was, but Fillmore was just too naturally dumb for that. Finally he got himself elected Senator though, when a couple of dozen extra ballots from Boot Hill turned up!"

"Sounds like he was a crook, sure enough, sir."

Hoppindorf lit up a dollar cigar and winked at me. "You've got a lot to learn about Foggy Bottom, my boy," he said, stepping aboard the VIP escalator. "He was a crook, all right, but a harmless one and hadn't even begun to learn his graft after four years in office. No, what happened to him was by purest accident."

The Marine at the door of the Senate War Club saluted Hoppindorf as we entered. The conference was still a few minutes away.

"An accident," he repeated. "It was an icy day in January. Most of Congress had stayed home to prepare for the inauguration a day

---

[12] William James had a brother, Clement, who believed he was the Pope. George's great-uncle Herbert disappeared in North Africa in 1932.

hence of the new President, Zachariah Tyler. The old man, James K. Pierce, had resigned the office at three that afternoon and taken a train to his home in Elmira. As a matter of Senatorial Preference, it was Poon of Kansas' turn to preside, *pro tem*, over the Committee of the Whole."

"You mean . . . ?" I was beginning to see the executive Chain of Command in action.

"Of course. The President and his Veep having left office, the job fell to the man who led the Senate — in this case, Poon, a fellow wholly unfit for anything more taxing than reading the Bible during anti-slavery filibusters."

"What on earth did he do, sir?" I exclaimed.

"Nothing! That's the thing of it! He slept! He slept soundly in his bed at the Republican Hotel on P Street throughout his entire term of office, which lasted nearly twenty-one hours. A slight case of Maryland malaria complicated by Irish whisky. No one ever told him he *was* President . . ."

Hoppendorf's voice trailed off in the echoing silence of the Club's War Room as the gaunt, tired man in the wheelchair appeared through a concealed doorway, trailed by three or four newsreel photographers.

Well, sir, George (*he said to me after a swallow of punch*), it was at that particular moment that I resolved to someday scale the mighty crags of power myself!

POLLYANNA VAN POON AND THE GENERAL

At the height of national enthusiasm for our country's revolutionary beginnings, George and I were asked to speak at surrealist ceremonies held within the hoary precincts of New York's Old Power Church. Located at Broad and Dorp Streets, the handsome 17th-century edifice seemed to provoke memories from my companion and he confided the following story to me on our slow ride "across town" after the ceremonies were concluded. Please note our 'Resident's sensitivity toward both sides in the civil conflict, once again demonstrating his keen political acumen and intense desire to avoid confrontation. (GLT)

You know (*George began*), if my Daddy had ever traveled anywhere, he would have come to New York City. First, because he always had a strong desire to visit the Stock Exchange and, second, a nearly equal wish to see Van Poon House, where George Washington met his Valley Forge.

Now, the Van Poons[13] are a branch of the family that sailed west from the Low Country about the time Manhattan was being bought for wooden nickels and pot-cheese from the Hohosmokit Indians, who of course didn't really own it. Dutch ducats made sure that Hendryk Van Poon *did* own the island himself only a few years later, but it was quickly lost in a game of nine-pins that Hendryk bowled with Adolph Rockefeller, a recent settler from Bavaria.[14]

Be that as it may, the Van Poons became the social paradigm of "Old Apple Town" in the years just before the so-called American

---

[13] The Van Poons are thought to be descended from Posett Boozeman, the grand-daughter of Sackville Boozeman, an actor in the notorious Fyrsygn Theatre of Lerndon. Posett's twin sister Canary married "Crazy Chester" Poon and later immigrated to the American colonies. Possett, who had been living with the couple, fled in hysteria to Delft, formed an alliance with a wealthy fish broker and followed (pursued?) Canary and Chester to America about 1705. GGP's version of the story is romantic but incorrect.

[14] Hendryk Van Poon and Adolph Rockefeller are well-known characters from Albany Courtland's comic memoirs "Dog Days Among the Dutch" and "Ichorbocher Irving's Wit."

Revolution. Their commodious, pilloried mansion sat like a fashionable hat-box upon the summit of Cobbs's Hill, which was the highest point between Lower Wall and the swampy Killkill River.

By 1776, its occupants were Marcus Van Poon, a rather stuffy hardware importer, getting on in years, and his wife, the former Pollyanna Uptown, a renowned beauty, still in her early twenties. Van Poon House was known for its parties, teas and frequent balls, and so was Pollyanna Van Poon. It was this remarkable lady who very nearly "turned the rebel tide" on a warm fall afternoon two hundred years ago.

The lovely Pollyanna[15] was, naturally, a loyal Colonial American. Her wealth, position and breeding dictated that she should despise the idle mobs that followed rabble-rousers like Sam'l Adams (a former tax-collector who had been caught "skinny-dipping" the King's accounts) or the suicidal land-speculator, Patrick Henry.

It came, then, as an unexpected surprise when she sent her servant-girl Porcelain down to General Washington's encampment near Crook's Landing, only about three blocks away.

Washington's Third Tatterdemalion Militia was then engaged in the confused pursuit of Lord Pinguid's Cornish Sappers, both armies having become lost when a sudden squall had deprived them of both their maps and their collective footing. The British troops recovered nicely by sending their uniforms out to be cleaned, while their Generals took brunch in Brooklyn.

Washington's men, however, had no uniforms and so took solace in eating whatever rabbits, chickens or apple pies managed to come their way. The American Commander himself was about to dine on warm groatcakes and warmer ale when the sultry Porcelain knocked on his tent-flap and was admitted by the sentry.

"General Washington, sir, my mistress, Miz Van Poon'd like to have you for lunch," said Porcelain with a graceful Caribbean courtesy.

"My dear," remarked the General, brushing off his cocked hat, "I wouldn't at all mind having *you* for lunch!"

---

[15] Uptown (or Upton) was a traditional name from the Umberland Counties of England. In Manhattan to this day natives refer to anything north of Wall and Bush as "uptown" — classy and high-rent.

"You better keep your ol' walrus teeth away from me, soldier-man, cause I ain't some Verginnie slave-gal you can knock over behind your woodpile!" Porcelain responded.

The General was cogitating the effect of this kind of sentiment on his nascent republic when Porcelain coyly flashed her apron and added, "Save it for later in the afternoon, up on The Hill."

Washington made sure his men were busy at work (printing up more Liberty Money so they could "buy" supplies), changed into his other uniform and rode his white charger "Excess" up the maple-shaded lane to the door of Van Poon House.

The clever Pollyanna had prepared a number of tasty distractions for our unwary Commander, who had no idea that Redcoats Lord Pinguid, General Fitzgeorgewallis and dashing young Earl Whigg were gathering their forces into precise geometrical formations for a bold retreat north into Connecticut.

If, in the steamy late afternoon, Washington had chosen to look out of Pollyanna's upstairs bedroom window (which he did not) he would have seen the splendid columns of red, white and blue disappearing up the dusty road toward Harlem.

"Do stay a bit longer, you *sweet* man," cooed Pollyanna to George as Porcelain brought tea and truffles. "My husband is in town with his needles and nails and knives and never comes home 'til six!" She playfully snatched his wig from his head and hid it under her ample petticoats.

"Just as you say, M'am," replied George, pursuing her from the room. "You make me feel like a Liberty Boy again!"

The Liberty Boys themselves had mostly gone home with the money they had just made, or else were drunk on liberated Yankee brandy by the time their exhausted General returned to camp.

"General! General!" shouted Washington's aide-de-camp. "The damned Hessians have made off behind our backs! There's no hope of trimming their tailcoats before Winter! Our Sacred Cause is in grave peril!"

Immediately, the resolute Commander made his decision. He would move his personal Headquarters up to Van Poon House for the duration of the social season, or until his officers could round up enough unemployed locals to make a new Militia, whichever came first.

Yet, even the beautiful and persistent Pollyanna could not, in time, prevent the traditional ignorance of the Colonial Office from losing the American War. Despite her attempts to keep him occupied, Washington and his army prevailed at the Battle of Caesar's Heights and the King's Men surrendered.

In her later years, when the city had grown nearly all around the base of Cobb's Hill, Pollyanna Van Poon often sat rocking in her upstairs window, remembering the bloody battle she had once prevented and caressing a cherished souvenir of those difficult days — General Washington's off-white horsehair wig.

That very wig is still on view in the Van Poon House and for obvious reasons of family tradition, my Daddy had a fascination for it. Alas, though — he never did see the wig itself. His curiosity had been piqued by a sepia-toned photograph of the by then shapeless artifact in the National Geographic.[16] My Daddy had cut this page from the magazine and kept it tacked to his workshop door for many years.

---

16 "Colonial Curiosities in Old Manhattan," in the October 1934 issue.

JEAN LE POON, PIRATE-PATRIOT

George told me this next story to keep my mind occupied and stomach calmed during an especially long delay in our flight to attend the Nat'l Surrealist Party Convention of '76. I was suffering from a touch of air-sickness, the small plane was stuffy and it seemed as if we would never arrive at our destination. As he so often does, our 'Resident found an amusing parallel to the immediate situation, and set about to reveal it in a most indirect way . . . (GLT)

Back in 1936 (*George mused*), when the whole civilized world was busy wondering how the movie about the King Who Fell in Love was going to turn out, I was a young, scrub-headed mail-jockey, flying a dusty Gnome-Wasp 1773-B bi-plane back and forth across the Ruby Mountains of Nevada.

It was damn cold, I can tell you, sitting in that open cockpit at a hundred m.p.h. Besides, there being less than a hundred-thousand souls in the whole state, it could be a pretty dull life for a boy who liked to listen to swing-music on "Your Hit Parade."

So it was that I came to jump all the puddles, fences and cows between Winnemucca and New Orleans, on the suggestion of my big-city cousin Harry Cox,[17] who worked for the newsreels, liked to buzz around Las Vegas and who now wanted to cover the Mardi Gras.

"Fly me down, Georgie! We'll have a party! Everything's on the expense account!" he said. And added, "Whoopee!"

We scuzzed and bumped over the Great Southwest for a couple of days, past Nugget and Nowhere and Wretched and finally touched down at Big Swamp Field, ready for bourbon and blues. It was a memorable Southern holiday! We signed Irving Thalberg's

---

[17] Harry Cox, Jr. (his parents were Sylvestor "Harry" Cox, brother to GGP's mother Mamie, and Lorna Porter, a timber heiress) moved to Heater, California in the mid-Sixties where he produced records and collected alternate realities for his Nude Age Enterprises. He coined the phrase "Everything you know is wrong," which has been pirated by unscrupulous publishers ever since.

name on every bill that came our way for the next week, until the studio called Harry and told him to "take his lens cap and stick it where the lamps don't shine."

I had to be back to fly the mail to Carson City only a day off schedule as it was, so we began the return trip with Harry pretty gloomy about probably losing his job. I tried to cheer him up with some swing music on my kazoo. That made him gloomier, so I hit on the trick of telling him about my long-lost Louisiana ancestor, Jean Le Poon,[18] a pirate who made his headquarters on Rat Island down in the Mississippi marshlands.

"That man wasn't any more a Frenchman than my Daddy's hat," I shouted to Harry over the roar of the 12-cylinder engine. "He was a runaway, who later married a quadroon girl named Voodoo Annie. She knew everything about those swamps down there and the two of them got practically an army of hot-bloods together to raid Spanish ships and deal in slaves."

"I'm either hungry or airsick!" yelled back poor Harry.

"Don't worry, just listen! Now, this Le Poon was a real buccaneer and the last of the breed, too, because this was around 1810 and the Old Days were about gone — just like always."

Harry said nothing.

"We were down on Rue Le Poon for the big parade on Tuesday," I continued, "and that reminded me of the story about him and General Andrew Jackass, the Indian-killer, who later became the first Wooden President."

"I gotta go!" yelled Harry.

"They won't let you over Texas," I replied. "You'll have to wait until we're close to Albuquerque. Concentrate on the story and it'll help. Now, all this happened about the end of the War of 1812. The Red Coats had burnt down the White House. A full fleet-load of 'em was ready to invade New Orleans. A desperate situation! Le Poon wrote a letter to the Governor offering his pirate army's aid in the crisis. General Jackass came down South for a secret meeting. Naturally, it was agreed the U.S. needed the pirate's help. Imagine

---

[18] "Jean le Poon" may have been a son of Isaac Poon, whose later years are unknown. The oldest of the Five Poon Brothers, Isaac was a gun-runner for Indian Militia units in and around the Mississippi Delta during the Revolution.

the arrangement — like having Capone's mob join the Marines to fight the Canadians who're attacking Chicago."

"What are you talking about? Land by the side of the road!"

"Won't be long now," I replied, and continued, "So Le Poon called all his buccaneers together and sent them out into the swamps. These fellas didn't know much about the U. S. of A., but they loved to fight dirty!

"Well, news traveled real slow in those days, so it was a few months after the War was supposed to be over that the big battle came between the privateers and the Brits. Of course, the pirates hid behind stumps and routed the Redcoats who, true to form, expected the enemy to behave like gents instead of skeeters!

"After the victory, the Governor threw a big party and Le Poon came with Voodoo Annie and caused quite a stir when he insisted that he exchange partners with General Jackass and then did the Swamp Stomp with the General's lady, while Annie kept the General mesmerized on the verandah."

"Where are we now . . . ?"

"Almost there, Harry. Remember, this man was a hero and had a right to be pardoned for all his past crimes. But the perfidious Yankee Generals took his ships and every barrel on the docks as soon as they moved in. Told him it was all stolen property, which it was, twice or three times over. Le Poon got away by night and turned up down on Margarita island off of Texas where he used Spanish gold to build an outlaw town. Caused a lot of trouble before the Navy burned it down. After that, Jean Le Poon vanished into the mangroves."

I was about to go on to tell Harry about several other romantic legends connected with my ancestor when Gorgon Field came over the horizon and I had to land for gas.

Ironically, the outcome of this Mardi Gras adventure was that I was fired from the Air Mail Service for unauthorized use of the Gnome-Wasp and spent the next year doing stunts at county fairs, while my erstwhile friend and relation Harry Cox returned to Hollywood, sold Errol Flynn on playing Jean Le Poon in "The Pirate-Patriot," stayed on the studio payroll and enjoyed considerable success before becoming a war correspondent in 1943.

Harry and I met occasionally on both sides of the Hump during the dark years of the War and, at Yalta, over bad Balkan beer and good Iranian caviar, he finally thanked me for the inspiration for his first Hollywood success.

"It wasn't the story itself so much as the way you sold it, Georgie! Kept me stuck to my seat! I truly meant to cut you in on the thing somewhere, but it just took off too fast."

"No need to apologize, Harry," I said. "The Poon Family heritage belongs to all Americans!"

TOPEKA POON — AMERICAN INVENTOR

'Resident Papoon delights in retelling the stories his father passed on to him more than fifty years ago. A far-away look will mist into his eyes and he will take on both the gruff but kindly voice of the elder George G. and the youthful tones of the boy he used to be. Here's one George loved to perform on the Grass Roots Tour and which got televised closed-circuit from the annual Pottsylvania Swiss Picnic in Glendale, California. (GLT)

One of the fine things (*George began as the pies were going around the picnic tables*) about growing up in "The Old Days" was that people remembered something besides what they saw over the TV. I know you've all noticed. It often seems to me that everybody started to lose their memories beginning about 1950. But anyway, my Daddy knew what *his* Daddy knew. Things like how to tell it was going to hail two days before it did, or how to make a chair out of a tree, or what became of our ancestral Poons.

One June afternoon in the late 1920s, my Daddy, my brother Dave and I were fishing down on the Poon River. We were using cheese for bait — the processed American kind — but the fish were asleep. So was I, nearly, when Daddy spoke up.

"Bet you didn't know this kind of cheese was almost called 'Poon-Cheese,'" he said.

"Aw, go on!"

"It's true! Before this cheese was invented, there was only them native-type cheese-balls. Always hard as a nut in wintertime and you couldn't hold onta one in the summer! It was a terrible problem, I can tell you! There was many men who'd worked years to try and invent some way to keep cheese from always fallin' apart and turnin' green. Then Topeka Poon[19] come along."

Brother Dave said, "My bait is fallin' apart and the fish keep

---

[19] Topeka Poon (1829-1871) is a very indirect relation of the Papoon family, being descended from a late arrival, Ben Poon of Rupshire, England.

eatin' it," and he hooked another hunk and dropped it over the side of the bridge.

"Well, that was a big concern back in Topeka's time, too, which was about the middle of the last century or so. He was a poor country boy, but had a natural knack with gadgets and tinkerin'. Took a look at the cheese industry when he was a young man and thought he could pick things up a mite.

"At that time only Frenchmen and New Yorkers ever bought cheese. Topeka, he thought if he could find a way to make cheese last longer and stay the same color, he could sell it to the poor and get to be rich himself! But years went by and he only got poorer.

Finally he couldn't get no poorer and was put in prison. His wife and children'd come to see him every week and slip bites o' cheese in through the bars. It was pathetic!

"Then one day a big cheese merchant who'd heard about his experiments gave him a hundred dollars to bail him out, so's he could get back to work on some new scheme.

"At the time, he was mixin' sulfur and lime with it, but that didn't do nothin' but spoil the taste. One winter night, as he was workin' over a hot cookstove, whippin' up fresh cheese and fixin' supper at the same time, a drop o' glop landed smack on top o' the hunk of buffalo burger he had sizzlin' in the skillet!"

My brother Dave, quick as a flash says, "You're tellin' us he invented the cheeseburger?"

And Daddy replied, "A lesser man might've stopped right there. Stopped and et his fill. But Topeka couldn't. He tossed some sand and salt and soda into that new batch and watched it firm up. Then he sliced it into slabs and took it off to the rich merchant.

"'Thank the Good Lord,' said Topeka. 'I have found a process whereby to make a true American cheese!'

"Well, I was just a kid and I wanted to know if it made Topeka Poon a lot of money and could we get some of it. My Daddy said to me, 'Not on your Gramma's tintype!' That crafty old fox got the whole invention, skillet included, for the hundred dollars bail money and Topeka was a broken man. Afterwards, he took to wearing suits and shoes made outta his processed cheese. Yep. He had a cheese hat that never melted in the sun or froze up in the snow, but he never had a penny in his poke, which was probably just as well, 'cause he was a man as crazed as your Uncle Sylvester[20] on your Mother's side."

"As bad as that?" I said.

"Died of rum and jungle fever down in Guatamala, looking for a cheese substitute."

Brother Dave said, "Why don't we just give this stuff to the fish all at once, instead of feedin' 'em by mouthfuls?"

Well, ladies and gentlemen, that's exactly what we did, then we walked across the Poon River Bridge and up the cart-track to home.

Thank you and good luck to all you Pottsyvanian Swiss and all-American friends!

---

[20] Sylvestor was always known as "Harry." His son, named "Harry" is known as "Happy." Sylvester died of rum and jungle fever in the Upper Sandusky.

MAJOR ZEPADIAH POON, EXPLORER

Here's another infamous Poon, always a standard item in George's repertory, especially fascinating to college audiences, with its references to "alternate realities" mysteriously created by Western Indians. This version is the one he told at the 1976 Solid State College commencement, where George was awarded an Honorary Doctorate of 'Pataphysics and Natural Surrealism. (GLT)

Up until about 175 years ago (*George began*), most folks had a terrific fear of anything bigger, deeper, wider or taller than what they were used to back home in Europe or in the worn-down hills of New England. It took a strong man in a tough pair of pants to take a fancy to the fantastical horizons beyond the Ol' Miz Sip, where herds of mammoths, crystal mountains and nations of dwarves were thought to abide.

A few rugged fellows, sick of civilization even in those uncivilized times, had gone alone into the wilderness in search of beauties and beavers. The undercover expedition of "Badweather" Lewis and "Griddley Bear" Clark had gone forth to infect the Indians with a fatal dose of progress. By 18-and-ought-six, the sultry town of St. Louis was beginning to fill with others of the breed, waiting for the first opportunity to make a pile and move into a house with air-conditioning.

It was as if the seething river-bottom community was a launching pad and the distant Rockyfella Mountains were the surface of the Moon, pocked with a few fresh footsteps and soon to be littered with the castoffs and debris of exploration.

Major Zepadiah "Ol' Zep" Poon,[21] an uncle of my mother's daddy, was stationed in those days at Fort Ferocious as an Injun Giver. Unqualified as he seemed for trailblazing, being cursed with an inverted sense of direction and terrible spelling, Ol' Zep and his

---

[21] Ol' Zep married three times, but since his five children were all girls, the family name was lost. Two of the girls, Elma and Wilma married bothers, Wilmer and Elmer Fudd. (See *Woots* by Julius Fudd, Doubledare, NY 1976.)

men marched along the Miserable River into the Great Plains, where they encountered the Left Feet Indians.

Following orders, the soldiers first shot off their guns to get the attention of the natives, who were given to speaking among themselves in a foreign language instead of listening politely to the speech Ol' Zep delivered, which went something like this: "My children. Big Chief All-Men-Created-Equal promises peace and protection. He can protect his children best if they do not interfere with his plans. This land cost many buckets of money. Learn how to spend it."

Then he gave each Indian a piece of silver with the President's picture on it, bearing the inscription "Good for One Free Ride," and a small bottle of aftershave.

Moving slowly upstream, the solders treated similarly with the Gnat, the Skeeter and the Chigger Indians, who swarmed around their canoes like flies. At last, following what is now known as the Poon River of Kansas, they could see snowy peaks in the distance. They had reached the foothills of the great "Rocky" Mountains. One towering height stood out from the others a few miles ahead.

Having seen this awesome sight, Ol' Zep declared to his men that he would climb to the mountain's top in order to survey the surrounding country. Already exhausted by the Wonders of the West, his men thought he was touched by "Injun Fever," but could not dissuade him from his new adventure.

Ol' Zep set out on what seemed to be a simple excursion of a few days. He rode his nimble pony up the slopes for half-a-week, then climbed on foot for two days more. He had come many miles from the last camp and yet the mountain seemed as far away as ever. In fact, it seemed even more remote and inaccessible.

Trying another route, the weary officer attempted a surprise assault upon the glistening white summit that rose tantalizingly before him. After another week, he was actually further away from it then when he started.

Of course, we now know that "Poon's Peak" was actually a Native American trick, much like the notorious "dry lakes" of the Great Southwest, designed to confuse the simple-minded white men and thus protect the natural environment. Ol' Zep never caught on to the simplicity of the illusion. He wrote in his Journal: "Dammed be this m'tn fer I hav tryd my wust and am cornvinsed no human bean cld assend unto its pinuckle."[22]

Gathering his men once more, Ol' Zep followed a fur trader's trail along the Lower Mud River, portaged past Skunk Rapids and finally lost himself in "Poon's Hell," now Idaho's Surrealist Nat'l Park. Here they found themselves in hot water, stumbling among a steamy assortment of geysers, sinks, pits, caves and spas. Reduced to pathetic circumstances, the desperate men wandered on, eating nothing but birchbark, bearfat and boots until they stumbled into Beaver Hat, a tiny community of saloons and cribbage parlors on the South Fork of the Forked River.

There the soldiers gradually recovered from their ordeal. Ol' Zep, after listening to the stories of the local mountain men (who stayed drunk in Beaver Hat nine months of the year), collected enough spurious information to write a book, which was published in the East after he was mustered out of the Army in 1810. The volume, obviously fictional, described the rich pueblos of New Mexico and the utter gullibility of the natives there and inspired many a horse trader to make the trek to Santa Fe, where he would immediately be thrown in jail.

As for Ol' Zepadiah Poon, he went into business making military uniforms for the Indians, who would often come through St. Louis on their way to Washington and who wanted to be togged out in the height of style. He lived long enough to see the great Territory he had helped to explore annexed to the Immortal Union, which got its "buckets of money" back with interest. And then some.

---

[22] *The Fictional Journals of Zepadiah Poon*, edited by Bro. Andrew X. Heebeejeebee, St. Mysrey's Press, Baltimore, 1961.

THE LIKELY STORY OF DUDLEY POON

I was fortunate to capture on tape the long reminiscence which follows. It was made during a vacation retreat in the Big Sur country of California, where George and Mrs. Papoon unwound from their Campoon chores and early months in office. The 'Resident exchanged views with me and others of his close advisors and relaxed at night with brandy, cigars and story-telling. The adventures of Dudley Poon, George's distant but direct forbear, may be the most incredible of all his tales. It certainly challenges certain conventional views of continental exploration. Here's the way George told it . . . (GLT)

It was my Grandaddy Poon who told this story to my Daddy, George Papoon Sr., who told it to me about fifty years ago on a late afternoon in August, when the wheat fields stretched out toward the horizon and the sunset was almost butter-yellow. We sat together that day on the porch of the Papoon homestead in Poonton, Kansas, where I was born, we drank lemonade and we swapped lies.

"I bet I could swim to the bottom of the Lime Pond and catch that ol' fish with my hands," I said.

"I bet you don't," my Daddy said. "'Cause that ol' boy is bigger 'n you are, I expect."

A breeze was starting up over the yellow-grey landscape that spread out from the homestead. "Tell me another of Grandaddy's stories," I said.

My Dad lit a tailor-made, put his feet up on the railing and blew me a smoke ring. His Daddy's memories reached a long ways back. Old William James had been born in 1799 and he had heard a lot from *his* father, who was one of the Poon brothers of Kentucky, born in pre-Revolutionary days.

"How long you figure our line's been hunkerin' down over a piece of this American soil?" my Daddy asked me.

Part Three: The Roots of Poon

"Gee, I know about the big war between the Poons and the Gumps down t'home in the Coal Hills," I said.

"That was nothin'," Daddy laughed. "That was only about a hundred years ago."

"How about Jeremiah Poon[23] and the Griddley Bear?"

"Now you're gettin' back there," my Daddy said, filling up our frosted glasses. I listened to the ice crackle. Crickets and frogs were singing and I put a pillow from the glider against the stoop and lay back and waited.

"Who was the first of the Poons?" I asked, after I'd waited long enough. Daddy blew me another smoke ring and flicked the ash into Mother's tea roses.

"The first Poon," he said, "was like your Uncle Herbert."[24]

"An undertaker?" I asked.

"No, indeed. A Californian."

Now, in those days California was thought of as the Land of Golden Winters. A Paradise. A place of earthquakes and artichokes. If there had been a time before movie cowboys and bathing beauties, I didn't know about it.

"During the Gold Rush?" I guessed.

"No, boy! I'm talking about your great-great-great etcetera Grandaddy Dudley Poon, who was the first so-called white man to take up a home in California and later walk clear across the Nation!"

"Gosh-all-fish-hooks!" I was excited. I knew that my grandfolks had been involved with some pretty exciting moments in history, but I never heard that I had a relative who was the first all-American.

---

[23] Pegasus Poon and his wife Patience were among the early pioneers into western Kentucky. They had five sons, Isaac (1759-?), Jeremiah (1761-1798), Zepediah (1766-1844), Yukaipah (1769-1812) and Daniel (1770-1858). The older brothers had seventeen children between them, accounting for the many Poon relatives not mentioned in these footnotes. It is from Daniel Poon that George G. Papoon is descended. Daniel married Nancy Noop in 1798. The next year a son was born, William James (1799-1882). Twenty-nine years later another son was born, Clement C. Poon (1828-1909). William James was so much older than his brother that people took to calling him "Pa" Poon and, after his father's death, he legally changed his last name to Papoon. William James Papoon was GGP's grandfather.

[24] True enough, Herbert Papoon was an undertaker and inventor. His "Seel'em" Brand casket glue revolutionized the business.

"That's right," my Daddy went on. "There was nothin' but Indians from coast-to-coast in them days. Ol' Chris Colombo, he never got farther than some o' them Caribbean resorts and even though there were always some Spaniards or Frenchmen out pokin' around, it wasn't until 1579 that a man who could speak the King's English settled down for a while.

"Now that man was an ancestral Poon! Dudley Poon his name was, a young man — not too much older'n you, boy." Daddy reached down and tousled my hair. "This story goes way back now, and it was my Daddy's daddy that told it to him, but it's true history all the same. It's written up as a footnote in the history books."

I remember how warm that night was. Daddy had to speak up over the humming and chirping of the night-bugs.

"Now, this Dudley Poon was the youngest of four brothers. Their father was a big land-owner over in England when they had Queen Elizabeth. He was a strong-headed boy and liked to fool around too much with all the farm girls thereabouts."

"Like Brother Dave," I said.

"Worse! But they sent him away down to London, England, when he was only fourteen, to get some schoolin'. Didn't take him long to find out about wine, 'n' older women, 'n' bein' a play-actor! He joined up with a bunch o' boys who worked for a Duke and they'd go around and do plays for the rich folks.

"Well, young Dud got himself mixed up in some kind of scrape. Probably had to do with the ladies, but the story was never told. He turned up a couple of years later or so as an actor at a big barn of a place where they did comedies and vaudeville for the city people."

"Like we see at Keith's over in Lincoln?"

"Somethin' like, but the audience in this theatre was always real rowdy and boozed up. They liked a good fight in those days. As a matter of fact, they used to put big fightin' dogs up against griddley bears in the place next door, for the folks who like a little sport.

"It happened one day that a bear so scared the dog that come up against him that the dog run off. The crowd went chasin' after him and got into a knock-down brawl with the folks who were tryin' to watch the play. Dudley and the other actors tried to go on with the show, but there was strange men suddenly tryin' to sword-fight with 'em! Things got so fierce that Dudley had to run one big fella through with his sword!"

"He musta been a regular Doug Fairbanks!"

"Well, that's just what it was like, boy. The Sheriff and his men were after him then, chasin' him through the streets, and he just slipped past 'em in time and made his way down to the river where the docks were.

"Now, Dudley was real smart. He was actin' the part of a sailor in the play, so he was dressed to fit in with the hustle 'n' bustle. Made his way to where there was three handsome ships at anchor 'cause he knew this was the fleet of the famous pirate, Sir Francis Duck!"

"A real buccaneer?"

"You betcha, boy! This Cap'n Duck was only a boot-heel taller 'n four feet, but he was a terror of the ol' Spanish Main. Brought back trunks full 'o gold 'n' pearls for the Queen. Now he was about to set sail again, around the Horn, lookin' for treasure with these three ships.

"Well, sir, Dudley knew that the constables were close behind him, so he picked up a big wheel o' cheese and joined in a line of men who were loadin' provisions aboard *The Gold Behind*, which was Cap'n Duck's personal flagship.

"He was in a hurry, and it was at that moment Dudley Poon decided he was ripe to seek his fortune where the pickin's looked better and he joined up to be a pirate himself."

Daddy paused. "I'd better make this story short. Don't want to talk through supper."

I could smell chicken frying back in the kitchen, where my Mother was whistling an old song.

"No chance of that," I said. "I'm too hungry. Go on!"

"Well, I'll skip past the months the pirate ships spent sailin' across to the shores of Brazil," Daddy continued. "But one fine mornin', Dudley was standin' his watch when he sees a flock 'o green birds come chatterin' down and settle on the spars like crows in a corn-patch. Then he saw land not too far off and pretty soon they sailed into a deserted bay, stocked up on fruits and fresh meat and, a week or so later, they set off again South and around the Horn.

"You must've read how the wind always storms down thataway and how the water's full o' icebergs and how all them little islands can confuse a man so's he don't know where to go. Well, one of Cap'n Duck's little boats ran aground and sank and another one had a mutiny and turned tail for the tropics. Only the *Behind* made it through to the Pacific and I don't have to tell you, most o' them sailors thought they'd never see home again.

"But then the weather began to warm up some and it wasn't too long before they began to meet some Spanish treasure boats, loaded up with silver, jade 'n' moonstones. It didn't take much more 'n a couple of cannon-shot and a show o' force to take 'em and then a few little port-towns into the bargain.

"In those days, the Spaniards was meltin' down silver and gold trinkets the Indians had saved up for centuries and shippin' them off to home in tubs. Ol' Cap'n Duck and his men finally got so much loot aboard that there was hardly room left for food and water, so he decided now was the time to make back for England."

"Around the Horn again?"

"No, siree, boy! That Crazy Duck sailed straight North, trying to find a way around the top o' the continent. He thought there was clear sailin' right across Canada! So they passed up the tropics 'n' the deserts and came right spang into a big fogbank that never did seem to have an end. They sailed right on past California and the weather got so cold that the men had to sit on each other's feet to keep them from freezin'!"

"Gosh!"

"Still, Cap'n Duck kept pokin' around in one useless bay after another to try and find one that kept on goin' East. After about a month, one dark night the crew came around knockin' on his cabin door and suggested it might be time to head on down to the South Seas. Dudley Poon spoke up for the sailors, 'cause of his natural actin' abilities, and pretty soon the Cap'n agreed, mostly because he was as cold as everybody else.

"But *The Gold Behind* had sprung a few leaks, so they put her in at a place where they could run her up on the sand and fix her hull. That place was near San Francisco, California, so they still needed all the driftwood they could gather up to keep warm. After that they pitched their tents inside a wooden fort to keep 'em safe from the Indians and started work on patchin' up the *Behind*."

"Was these Indians Apaches?" I wanted to know.

"Relatives," my Daddy answered. "And it wasn't but a few hours 'til the first Indian come walkin' up over a sand-dune and started in to yell at 'em. Dudley and the rest of the sailors thought they were in for a fight, but this fella just wanted to talk. He talked for a couple of hours, and of course Dudley didn't understand a word and just went on workin'.

"So this Indian Chief come back every day to stand up on the hill and talk to the men while they worked. Young Dud got to listenin', and one night he started dreamin' about a great land that stretched on past the fogs to a high wall o' mountains and past them into dry deserts and then into ranges that was covered with snow all year. He'd be flyin' over those mountains and then wake up to hear the waves of the ocean poundin' up on the shore where they was camped.

"And that tide 'd come in and Dudley 'd dream about what the Indians said. How from the tops of these mountains you could see across a great plain, filled up with game and cut through by a river bigger 'n he could imagine. He took to dreamin' almost every night about this country and how the Red Man moved easy across it, doin' business and carryin' messages."

"What kind of a dream was that, Daddy?"

"Must've been a powerful dream, 'cause when Cap'n Duck was ready to sail on, 'round the world t' home, Dudley stayed behind and hid in the sand-dunes. Then, when the ship moved off on the tide, he joined up with a bunch of Indians and they all went up to the top of a cliff lookin' out over the ocean. The Indians built a couple of big fires and threw sagebrush on top to make 'em smoke good. Pretty soon that little boat disappeared into the fog and Dudley was all alone — the only professional actor in all of America!"

"Wash hands for supper!" my Mother said, poking her head out past the screen door. "My, it's cool out here! That kitchen's a furnace tonight."

"What happened to ol' Dudley Poon then?" I asked.

Daddy took his feet down off the porch railing and started to roll up his shirt sleeves. "Took him twenty-five years to get home, walkin' all the way! Married an Indian princess and took up performin' some of his favorite plays at the native ceremonials.

"Managed to teach a few braves Latin and English and they teepee toured all across country. Ended up near Jamestown, booked passage home with his beautiful princess and got back to London where they both was the talk of the town."

"I'll bet!"

"And his adventures got written up in a Shakespeare play. You can read it in school if you've a mind to. Called 'A Poon's Dream.' Wasn't 'til a hundred years later that his grandson Chester Poon come over and he was the second of our family line in America."

"What was he known for?"

"I'll have to tell you about Crazy Chester[25] some other day, Junior," replied my Daddy. "Right now we got some eatin' to do!"

"I'm comin'," I said as he went inside. The screen door slammed behind him. Fireflies skimmed the lawn. My Mother's deep-fried chicken scented the air.

---

[25] "Crazy Chester," a noted eccentric, inventor and organist, lived with the twins Canary (1681-1732) and Possett (1681-1731) Boozeman. It is generally thought that Canary was the mother of Chester's heirs, twin sisters Calliope and Appolonia (born 1723) but not necessarily of son Pegasus (born 1720). Chester gave up the title Lord Poon upon emmigrating to the Carolina Colony.

Part Four

Not Insane!
Photo by Dr. W. Deadjellie

PART FOUR: "OFF THE WALL" | 139

"Off the Wall"

"FEATURING THE WIT AND WISDOM OF FIRESIGN THEATRE'S DAVID OSSMAN"

That's the way I was billed! Here are seven of the short pieces I wrote mostly in 1978 for the Santa Barbara News & Review, *plus one from* Crawdaddy *in the same year. Re-reading them in 2007 it was deja-vu all over again. Price of gas, pop culture, celebrity news, computers, general weirdness — it's all here! So I've conspired to muse again on these events as they seem now, seen from the 21st Century.*

1. FOOD CRIMES . . . 140
THE GOOD OLD DAYS OF EATING AND MEMORIES OF A SODA-JERK.

2. I CAN'T GO HOME, AGAIN . . . 143
FROM HOMESTEAD REMOVAL TO URBAN WATERCRESS IN L. A.

3. NEWS JUNKIE . . . 146
BRING ON THE NOW-A-GO-GO DISCO TV NEWS!

4. THE NIX A CLONE? . . . 150
HOW MANY OF HIM WERE THERE, REALLY?

5. ENCOUNTERS WITH DYLAN . . . 154
A FAN CAN ONLY GET SO CLOSE . . .

6. MICKEY'S BIRTHDAY PARTY . . . 157
THE ORIGINAL FRANCHISE MOVIE STAR GOES TO THE WHITE HOUSE.

7. FUTURESHOCK IN A BOX . . . 160
AND SO NERD CULTURE WAS BORN.

8. UFOVERDOSE . . . 163
FIREWALKERS! PYRAMID HATS! CRYSTAL SKULLS! IT'S ALL A CON!

FOOD CRIMES

Back in the Simmering Sixties, when many of us were singing "Where Have All the Flowers Gone?" and comparing the rise of Lyndon B. Nixon with that of Franklin D. Hitler, it was still possible to get a restaurant meal without accounting for one's personal share of the National Debt.

Now, of course, the tune is "Where Has All the Money Gone?" and anyone who remembers the Depression will tell you and me that, even if Things Were Bad, the price of food was right down there with a ten-cent ticket to the Bijou.

Even twenty years back, in the black-and-white glow of the mid-fifties, the price of a burger wasn't determined by how much gasoline it took to make it, but by the small change in the average person's pocketbook. (Remember "pocketbooks?")

As proof of the insane rise in food prices since the Big Gas War, allow me to take you out to a hypothetical meal at the local Woolworth, circa 1955. The McDonald's principle ("put it in plastic") not yet being in force, we will be sitting on Naugahide stools at the counter, eating off real plates and drinking out of real glasses.

What'll you have? A working-girl's Fountain Lunch? Swell. How about a large fresh orange juice, bacon-and-tomato toasted three-decker sandwich and a DeLuxe Tulip Sundae (two dippers of Ice Cream covered with Crushed Fruit or Fresh Fruits in Season, choice of strawberry, pineapple, cherry, chocolate or hot fudge. Topped with Whipped Cream, Pecans and Cherry Ring)? That'll do it? Good! Your tab is 85 cents. I'll leave a buck on the counter. The 15-cent tip won't go far, but at least the dime is mostly silver.

As for me, I can't resist today's Feature Number One — the Roast Turkey Dinner — Roast Young Tom Turkey, Celery Dressing and Giblet Gravy, Creamy Whipped Potatoes, Fresh Vegetable, Cranberry Sauce, Hot Roll and Butter. Even with a bowl of Fresh Homemade Vegetable Soup with Crisp Wafers and Lemon Meringue Pie at opposite ends, this spread will set me back only an unbelievable 95 centavos American. Rich or poor, a meal for under a buck. And I don't mean drowned "cobettes" and beakless cluck either!

Lest you think these low prices applied only to the Woolworth counter and that a class meal was worth (as it is today) a second mortgage on the condo or missing this month's payment on the Porsche, let me present you with the menu for Manhattan's justly renowned "21" Club (Havana cigars procurable by the box) for the evening of Friday, May 18, 1956. Let's order damn near one of everything and see what it sets us back.

For hors d'oeuvres, Cherrystone Clams (95 cents) and Paté of Chicken Livers "21" ($1.35). For potage et salade, Green Turtle Soup (90 cents) and Bibb Lettuce ($1) The entrée? The lady will have Brook Trout au Blue Mousseline ($3) and I'll take the Broiled Lamb Salisbury, Nicoise ($3). Legumes? French Fried Zucchini ($1), Yellow Squash (75 cents). Pomme? Baked Idaho (75 cents).

Let's go all out for dessert, because I have no idea at all what these tasties might be. I'll try the Kersen Aardbeien en ys Urk at $1.75, and you must try the Profitrolles au Chocolat ($1). We could hardly go wrong. And two coffees with cream (at 50 cents each).

Sans wine, this dinner for two, including cover charge and tip, comes to just over $20. Amazing!

The ultra-average Budd Bland family of Bozoville, USA, with its two-and-a-median children would spend that much to hunker down at Carrows on their way through Santa Barbara to visit Hearst Castle.

I can't resist mentioning some of the other items available on that "21" menu: things like Fried Mussels, French Mackeral in White Wine, Tomato Surprise, a cold Potage crème Senagalese, boiled Calf's Head Vinaigrette, Fresh Florida Corn, Pommes hashed in Cream, and Butterscotch Ice Cream.

By comparison, this burg's over-sized carte du jour seems endlessly limited to a diet of Sprouts and Ferns in White Wicker Sauce, el Especial Numero Dos with a Dos Equis, por favor, and that old favorite, Fried Foods with French, Blue Cheese or oil-and-vinegar. Coffee in a plastic bag to go. Sugar and soy, thanks.

One's memories of memorable pigouts and food crimes remain savory (or disgusting) for years. I recall thick-thick chocolate malts at Fifties drive-ins in Los Angeles, served on a metal tray outside your car window with lots of napkins and straws and a plate of genuine onion rings. There were the hamburgers at

Stinky's Roadhouse out beyond Claremont on Route 66 — they disintegrated as you ate them, so full were they of juices and sauces and fresh tomato and lettuce.

I vaguely recall too many forks and too much Dom Perignon at Le Pavillion with a famous Steel Magnate whose daughter was marrying my best friend.

And there were the fresh peas I de-podded and ate the fattest of on their route to hot water in my Mother's kitchen.

I had two great teenage jobs that involved me in an Eating Scene. One was as a fry-cook at a definitely non-chain hamburger stand. Hamburger stands are a vanishing breed, but you can still find them in the Big City and they always have great specialties, like enough chili to soil everything you're wearing no matter how many napkins you soak through, or perhaps a thick slice of raw onion and no questions asked.

The other job occupied me for a year as a soda-jerk (no cracks, please) as part of clerking in my neighborhood drugstore. That little pharmacy had a marble fountain counter and porcelain-handled pullers for the syrups and soda-water, just like in the Coke ads on the backs of old *National Geographics*. I could make hand-packed chocolate sundaes for myself, gushing with chunky pineapple syrup, heaped with fresh walnuts, bedecked with maraschino cherries and red die number two. Sneak a treat like that today and the boss would have you up for Grand Theft!

All that was, of course, before the Nutrition Revolution of the late 1970s. In my youth, people who took vitamins were kooks (remember Vitamin Flintheart of Dick Tracy fame?) and items like bran, wheat-germ and yogurt were strictly for the cultists and the nudists.

Nowadays, such folk are strictly attractive and athletic actors promoting health, happiness and high prices. Their Doppelgangers on the TV, also ever-so-cute and integrated and guaranteed honest by the Federal Poor Taste Commission, continue to sing jingles of praise for goods which consist entirely of chemicals dissolved in water or else puffed up with air.

It's the land of the Blands eating the bland. Or, as someone once said, "More sugar!"

CAUTION! HEAVY CUISINE CROSSING! (2007)

Nearly thirty years have passed, and nearly thirty-thousand mostly forgettable meals have passed too, right on through our systems and on out to the wide-open and ever-rising sea. In the bowels of the digestive process, the Good Guys have won, or something like it. No trans-fats in the cuchifritos on Upper Broadway and plenty of Wild Natural Green Things in that salad-in-a-plastic-box nobody gets at McDonald's.

Loyal Americans and those awful Chinese Commies check one-another's e-mails at the same high-tech coffee shop, disguised as a Meditational Environment.

Jug Sanapanoma has been replaced by two-buck Chuck at all the best body-painting parties. Even my Island supermarket offers organic Japanese eggplants from Mexico and little boxes of 100% raspberry juice for the kids' lunch.

Of course, that double-venti cuppa fairly-traded joe only returns loose change for a fiver and all the Best Restaurants sting you seven bucks for a glass of alcohol-flavored drink and forty Georges for a plate of veggie pasta. Water from Fiji or Upper Turkmenistan runs about a dollar a glass and we all need six glasses a day.

But what the hey! We can have kiwis and avocados and sag paneer in our own breakfast nooks anytime we like. Let's Eat!

I CAN'T GO HOME, AGAIN

Are they out to obliterate your past? They've sure junked a chunk of mine! My block of Central LA's University Avenue may not have been the set for "Meet Me In St. Louis," but it served as a homey imitation for a while. Now, it's gone.

It's not only that the crazy old house I lived in got torn down — even the new building that replaced my house ten years ago is gone. Not only have all the houses and yards on the surrounding blocks been removed, even the blocks themselves — streets and all! — are gone!

University Avenue in the late 1940s was a quiet, residential street connecting the staid USC campus with madcap Fraternity Row.

Sometimes, when the Trojans were winning and the beer was flowing, the whole neighborhood felt like a small college town full of temporarily crazed undergrads.

Within a block or two stood both the vast, extravagant Shrine Auditorium, where Sixth Graders were sent to hear opera, and the immensely domed Christian Science Church, where I stopped going to Sunday School.

Church and Auditorium are still solidly in place, but USC, like an out-flow of hot lava, has obliterated nearly everything else in its path. Twin rows of ultra-Seventies condo-style student residences now flank a featureless mall where my street once ran,

Its reality eliminated by realty, that street seemed to still move underground, like a natural creek now diverted into the sewers.

I'd spent a lot of time on the banks of this urban creek-street, starring in Errol Flynn movies, where the big date palm in front of my house doubled as a Sherwood Oak. That neighborhood may have been right in the middle of Los Angeles, but it had its secret trails and hideouts and as natural a geography as one could expect under the sway of Almighty Grid. No secrets there now, just security.

I drove around the block looking for the block. Fraternity Row still survives — a temporal hallucination at the edge of a Black Hole where actual co-eds unload actual station-wagons and move into Sorority houses. It was a TV re-run of a Fifties college musical. At the void's opposite edge, 32nd Street School, hardly recognizable, also survives. Bright, squatty, Space-age bungalows have mushroomed from the ruins of the demolished two-storey brick school building.

Beyond the "tasteful," tacky condos, the obliteration continues. More blocks have been leveled out for the "tasteful," tacky New Age Blandness of the University shopping center.

Past that, the old neighborhoods begin again, an almost abandoned desert town going to seed, its rivers or mines or life-forces dried up.

"Afraid of the dark," I thought. "These USC planners are Afraid of the Dark. They've used my street, my corner of the woods, to provide a concrete corridor of safety from bed to lab — from one well-lit island of civilization to another."

Co-existence of the City of the Past with the City of the Future is impossible. The City of the Future overflows and obliterates and makes things so easy to keep clean. The City of the Past begins immediately, so look out!

I took the long way to where I was going after that — North from USC and skirting the Latino streets next to Downtown, where the entire rolling landscape has been revised to suit Big Bucks Banks and Bureaucracy. I drove to the place where the concretely channeled LA River bites the edge of Griffith Park.

I was going to a spot where I knew the water still flowed directly from the earth. A long time ago, with an Indian guide who knew something of the territory, I was shown a spring which never dries, where the Caweng-na Village sat, between the paws of Bear Mountain. (All this may sound hokey, but it is, of course, true.)

And even though the condo-minimalists have erected a pyramid to the Great God Tan where not too many years ago Dark Canyon Creek trickled in its forgotten channel down to Burbank, the spring of Caweng-na still gurgles out of the same hillside.

The spring, situated by bizarre coincidence between the time-warp fantasies of Warner Bros., Universal and Forest Lawn, flows into a concrete sewer under the road. The drain and curb are draped with fresh, cold watercress. Just a few feet back, behind thick bushes, a pond spreads out, reeds and cat-tails growing on its marshy edges.

Just there, very near the spot where D.W. Griffith recreated the Civil War, only a tombstone's throw from where the Founder rebuilt Mount Vernon, directly opposite the simultaneous turrets of Camelot and Shangri-La, a bit of one of the oldest neighborhoods in the City of the Past remains intact.

When you can't go home again, thank heaven for some place to go home to instead.

I DON'T HEART L.A. (2007)

I'm less sentimental now in the 21st Century about my long-lost home in the *noir* L.A. of the late Forties. After all, I've been here on my Island for nearly 20 years — longer than I've lived any place else — and the endless reaches of "Southland" concrete wilderness have long since faded into the smog of memory, leaving only those gorgeous color postcards of sunsets over palms and the Pacific. If that precious "Indian" spring still burbles out of Dark Canyon, and I hope it does, it's unlikely that the millions of tourists bound for game shows at Warners and thrill rides at Universal will care to notice.

The fact is, the only L.A. we ever could have been sentimental about has been bloodily exposed, brutally murdered in HORRIFIC HEADLINES! And left to bleed white in the novels (and movies made from them) of James Ellroy.

I still do think fondly about my days in Edendale and Mixville — the little-known corners of the city limits where the movies actually were born. Tucked into the once barren hills just west of Downtown were the studios of Western hero Tom Mix and fledgling cartoonist Walt Disney. Behind razor wire near Glendale Boulevard lingered a small stone monument to Comedy. Why? Because the ancient Selig Company had once made movies there. Just down the street a vast, empty warehouse stood forgotten for years. It was once Mack Sennett's Keystone Comedy Company and the largest enclosed concrete stage in moviedom. Chaplin capered, Swanson emoted, Keaton remained stone-faced and the Kops clambered into Model A's and drove out the front gates and into the madcap back streets along the L.A. River. Who cared? Nobody. The City of the Angles moved on, leaving its past like pigeon droppings on the sidewalk.

NEWS JUNKIE

I admit to being a TV news junkie. I think I must have gotten hooked about the same time we landed on the Moon. The TV news was so simple in those days. There was Uncle Walter and "Goodnight-Chet-Goodnight-David" on the networks, and Los Angeles had Jerry Dunphey, who looked like a newscaster, but otherwise had no perceptible personality.

The Unpredictable Presidency and the Evening News had a stormy but stimulating relationship thereafter. After we went to the

Moon, we went to China and then we went to Hell.

News got better and better in the Seventies. Well, actually the news got worse but The News got showbiz. Taking its cue from the death of LIFE, the creative giants who develop news formats turned to PEOPLE. If Barbwa Walters can sell more Preparation H by talking to Sadat, Travolta and the Test Tube Mom all at once, why not?

These days, I can tune the tube in at 4:30 and, with clever manipulation of the knob, continue watching until the last network credits roll at 7:30. (On Fridays, I can stick with "Washington Week in Review" all the way to 8:00!)

I've grown to love the format changes down in LA. All new faces and new sets. They've redone CBS Studio A three times in four years. The current set looks like they intend to add a disco beat just as soon as they think we can take it, then bring on the dancers and strobes.

And the daily News Drama is "live" and full of soap-opera suspense. How can beautiful Connie Chung survive another insipid co-anchorperson? Will Jess Marlow really interview the leads in the fall lineup? Can Jerry Dunphey learn to ad lib? What happened to those sportscasters in plaid jackets who looked like they spent the day at Santa Anita?

Half of today's now-a-go-go newsmen have beards. One poor fellow on Channel 2 looks as if he glues his on, only to have the crepe hair begin to melt off under the hot lights.

All the ecological types who used to do gentle nature stories a few years ago have been replaced by ethnic types who do minicam reports on welfare frauds.

Kelly Lange, whose once-fashionable San Fernando Valley housewife look has been eclipsed by blazing Asian opposition, still survives, along with Dr. George.

The born-again blandness of the Carter administration is pretty well served by the current emphasis on personalities. Stories that could once have involved whole teams of producers, camera crews and newspeople can now be handled by one People File person and a still photo of Whoever projected on the Big Screen behind him.

A study by the American Medical Association claims that avid video watchers tend to be paranoid and pessimistic, whether from a heavy diet of reality or the junkfood of fiction. I wonder which program sells more handguns and Dobermans — "60 Minutes" or "Starsky & Hutch"?

Things must be getting worse in the rest of the world as well. In West Germany, Chancellor Schmidt recently urged families to shut off their TVs one day a week in order that they might talk to one another. "We have become more and more speechless and that frightens me," the Chancellor said.

The answer to all of that probably lies in being able to talk back to your TV. In one Ohio community, watchers can register their views on a system called QUBE. Given America's passion for majority rule, this may be the wave of the future. One TV, one vote.

Eventually, technology could give us the ability to do our own newscasts and broadcast them down the cable to friends and neighbors. "Good evening, this is the Jones Family News. In the headlines — Dad threatens to leave Mom after 32 years of married life. Heavy rains clog sewer — cleanout costs estimated at $75 to $100. A little later, we'll have a special report on the family finances and a look at Janey on her big date last night. But first, a word about . . ."

After all, does one's roof have to collapse in order to bask in the spotlight of video notoriety? Does one really need to know anything in order to have an opinion? Didn't Andy Warhol say that everybody could be famous, however briefly?

Perhaps when that day comes, when everything everywhere is equally important, then News junkes like me will be satisfied. Click, click, click . . .

CLICK, CLICK, OFF! (2007)

That day, I don't have to tell you, has come. I gave up being a News Junkie when the "pin-point" bombing began during the First Gulf Crusade. Drawn to the images of X-marks-the-spot destruction, I kept the TV tuned in until Mr. Rogers (of sainted memory) reminded us that those images were bad, really bad, for kids. Our two-year-old Orson couldn't have been happier when the bombing stopped at our house.

As for the Warhol Hole of Fame, instant celebrity burns brightly on the tube and computer screens 24/7. Celebrity available only through humiliation or excruciating competition (or both). The Trump lifestyle, with its comb-over cruelty, is available to the last butt standing, once a season. New York, meet Nero.

Local TV news still revels in the pseudo-excitement of "reporters" standing on freeway overpasses waiting for rain. Things can't get too bad for Channel Five Live.

Fox loves to bray contempt for the "elite," by which their loud-mouths mean anyone who sang along with "All You Need Is Love." CNN's face is busier with logos, multiple screens, running headlines and satellite savants than Times Square on New Year's Eve. No one can escape the embarrassment and brutality made possible by the hidden camera in somebody else's cell.

And yet, I don't have to tell you, the highest ratings for cable are nearly always for the wrestling shows — gigantic Macy balloons for phony violence — and that cartoon sponge, inexplicably potent at the bottom of the neighborhood sea.

On Easy Street
PHOTO BY DEBBIE GREEN

THE NIX A CLONE?

I once worked with a man who claimed that, as a baby, he had been kissed by the campaigning Franklin Delano Roosevelt prior to FDR's first election in 1931. As for me, the closest I've ever gotten to a Prez was last Rose Parade, where I had a keen view of the back of Gerald Ford's head. It was astonishingly bald!

I am, nevertheless, and thanks to TV, a President-watcher. Television glories in presenting the Prez, and never more so than during the regime of "RN," who invented something called "the Presidency" and liked to advertise it over the tube. Who can forget his phone call to the Moon? His trip to the Great Wall of Mars? His many good-byes?

Now, just when we wondered if we'd ever have the Old Nix to boot about anymore, he has surfaced from behind the walls of Spandau — er, San Clemente — to let us have another go at the World's Awkwardest Man.

As a matter of fact, for many years I was convinced that there was more than one "Richard Nixon." It seemed obvious that a mad medico in the hire of the CIA/Mafia Connection had cloned him sometime in the Fifties and with seriously defective results. How else might one explain the many photographs of him attempting simple manual tasks and failing so miserably?

Remember the time he got birthday cake all over his blazer and then let his dog lick it off? Or when he tried to adjust the microphone for Frank Sinatra? Sing "Home on the Range" with Pearl Bailey? And got bear-hugged by Sammy Davis? Were any of these the "real" RN? Could even Pat be absolutely certain?

Barring a clandestine clone, the only other reasonable explanation is a crypto-bionic simulation — something to be trotted out to shake hands, even if its hands never seemed to work right.

Occasionally, the simulation went berzerko, as when it tried to throttle House Doorkeep, "Fishbait" Miller. ("He grabbed me by the throat and was choking me. It was a hard grasp. I gasped for breath," said Fishbait.)

Once it mistook an Air Force Sergeant for something else — due to a bionic retina malfunction, I suppose. The following exchange was reported:

"Are you the boy's mother or grandmother?" Nixon asked the Sergeant.

"Neither," replied the man.

"Of course not," said Nixon and slapped the faithful Sarge on the cheek.

The Nix's most recent public appearance doesn't give one a lot of confidence that the duplicates have been dumped. A stewardess who served "him" during a flight to Washington this past winter said, "His eyes looked like in outer space!"

I haven't read the new Nixon memoirs and I don't suppose you have either. After hearing his cronies and camp-followers make their excuses, the epic of Crises 7 through 666 holds little in the way of reality for me. I was, in fact, delighted to see that the $20 book is not selling very well. (One book dealer reported that it had a "lousy binding." But then, The Nix always did have problems with his cover.)

Perhaps poor sales are partly due to the efforts of a Washington, D.C. group whose slogan is "Don't buy books from crooks." Two San Francisco women have even sued The Nix in an attempt to return some of the tome's potential profits to the Treasury, which, you'll remember, was repeatedly raided in order to build ever-higher walls around the Presidential Estates.

Actually, the only really newsworthy quote about the book I've come across is "former speechwriter" Patrick Buchanan's delightful prediction that the book "will be fully consistent with the truth." Analyze that sentence and you'll see why Nixon's speeches were so full of mesmerizing Double-Think.

And I'm sure the memoirs won't give us the really tasty Nixonian philosophy. On milk, for example: "Any kind of a thing, you can just, just a glass of milk. You don't have to talk with it or anything like that. It could be warm. It could be, uh, tepid, or it could be cold, but, uh, but it has a certain soothing effect. Uh, you could get people started on that."

Nixon's place in the polls depended on who you asked. My favorite was a sampling of patrons at Madame Tussaud's Waxworks in London, where he was chosen the third Most Fearful Figure, right behind Hitler and Mao — and just ahead of Jack the Ripper. I guess things like that — and having a brand of Egyptian hash named in your honor — can get a man down — even a President.

And, after the Fall, to suffer the indignity of having a Los Angeles freeway once named in one's honor changed back to Marina Freeway without so much as a dissenting vote — well, it could prove permanently damaging to the psyche. Assuming that a man who once said, "I can go into my office and pick up the telephone and in 25 minutes millions of people will be dead" has any psyche left.

Being a Natural Surrealist myself, I can see very little use to the Office of the President whatever. Constitutionally, his duties are limited to being Commander-in-Chief of the military and sundry other colorful but largely ceremonial responsibilities, along with the suggestion that he make recommendations to the Congress.

Modestly, I might propose that the next time we have a chance, instead of looking for a Big Strong Man for a Big Tough Job, we "lower our expectations" and find a modest fellow, easily frightened by loud noises and incapable of considering numbers over one million. Someone, above all, who has another job he likes better and which he longs to get back to.

NO SUCH LUCK (2007)

Now, in the midst of the "presidency" of Crusader King George and Dick the Super Crony, I've heard more than one of my generation long for the Good Old Nixon Years. "Even Nixon was better than this moron," bemoan some of us who now fondly remember the fun we had with a guy who took us along with him to the Forbidden City on the Moon and finally resigned in shame because, actually, he was a crook.

Wouldn't we prefer that hapless Capricorn so profoundly uncomfortable in his body to a cocksure Cancer who, instead of living close to his natural element, Water, has chosen instead the barren but oil-rich wastes of Texas where he can pretend to be a cowpoke?

I had hoped The Nix was the last President from the cheap-gray-suited, alcoholic Forties. But they gave him Agnew when at last he Came Back in "Nix III" in 1968. Agnew! Like, he was gone in a Maryland minute! So then they gave us the Number Three Man,

Ordinary Jerry, recently venerated for staying the GOP course. Nix helicoptered out, Ford drove in and Rocky rolled up. The Republican Dream! An unelected administration!

Interrupted by a Southern Governor.

Then, in a riled-up, gun-totin' case of Central Casting, we inherited the amiable Dutch Reagan as the stand-in for Duke Wayne and we got The Empty Eighties. And, yup, Papa Bush, set to be Set Up, was right there in our Star Warrior's ear.

Interrupted by a Southern Governor.

The dynastic evolution of the Administrative line is really important to the Hungry Ghosts who conspire to tell everyone what to do. Think of all those Kennedys who never were nor never will be President. The ascendant Wives of damaged political husbands, the Senators' Sons, the Brothers-in-Waiting. The Southern Governors!

Art Wholeflaffer, Practicing Nudist
PHOTO BY TYLER THORNTON

Richard Nixon's brother sold shoes or something, Jimmy Carter's drank beer. Not likely groomable. So the Ghosts settled for the Bushes. (There are more of them than the Bakers.) And the Bushes, unlike the Venerable Nix, he of the Expletive Deleted, intend to squat on the Awful Oval Office until they can sell the off-White House to a billionaire Inside Trader. As is.

Expletive Deleted.

ENCOUNTERS WITH DYLAN

When it came, of course I took the opportunity to see Bob Dylan's movie "Renaldo and Clara." Advance word of it hadn't been so hot, but cries of disappointment at Dylan's latest are a tradition. Anyway, I'm one of those people he's never let down. A fan.

To me, the movie was a musical and we don't get many of those nowadays. It had the same sort of silly romantic plot that any 1940s musical would have used. A plot to hang the songs and dances on — to give some sort of continuity to hot jive from the Goodman or Dorsey bands, Carmen Miranda, Roy Rogers, Spike Jones and lots of beautiful girls.

Except in "Renaldo and Clara" it was mostly just Dylan and only a couple of beautiful girls. An impersonation of a celebrity goes deeper than Steve Allen as the King of Swing. Bring on the real triangle and stand back for the musical numbers. How familiar they were — and yet re-dreamed and metamorphosed. Bob Dylan, still the poet laureate of the Natural Surrealists.

Like most people, I've never met Dylan, tho I was very close to him once. Also, probably like most people, I've had a lot of encounters with Dylan — encounters that stick in the mind, to be remembered whenever a familiar lyric appears.

The first time I ever heard a Dylan song, it was to play a request on a folk-music show I once DJ'd. I had to hunt around for that first "Bob Dylan" album, racked in among the old Woody Guthrie, Cisco Houston and Odetta albums, and all those Folkways records. I played "Highway 51" and kept the album closer to hand afterwards. (I pulled out my own copy of the album recently — so old it's in mono.)

Seven years later, over the newly hippified KMET, Peter Bergman and I played "I Want You," "Tom Thumb's Blues," "Don't Think Twice" and "I Am a Lonesome Hobo," along with "Savoy Truffle," "Sexy Sadie," the Stones and Ravi Shankar. A Dylan song always made the perfect segue.

Speaking of segues, the Firesign Theatre once wrote a half-hour radio play specifically to end with the line, "It's all over now, baby blue," and then to pop right into the song. (In our case, the lyric meant that Roman Emperor Caliyuga had succeeded in his mad dream to completely cover the Empire with tiles the color of his eyes — but you probably had to be there.)

Dylan was there (lyrically) when I performed my first comedy turn on a TV show. I played an elderly gentleman who went completely whacko while reading the words to "Maggie's Farm."

Some of Dylan's cronies were around our neighborhood in the late Sixties — particularly Phil Ochs, whose "The War Is Over" campaign was swept away by the first of many waves of LAPD. Always a little mad, Phil flared, burned out and suicided. Ramblin' Jack Eliot was around too — high on whatever was handy — always on, talking about boats and women. It was good to see Jack again in "Renaldo and Clara," unchanged. Along with Dylan, a survivor.

When the Firesign was first ushered into the presence of Columbia Records' charismatic president, Clive Davis, the boss, was on the phone with Dylan. (Either that, or Davis always used this ploy to impress newcomers.)

"Sure, Bob! Just great! Absolutely! I'll take care of it," said the president. I didn't know until I read Clive's book years later — after he had been fired for paying for his son's bar-mitzvah out of company lunch money — that Dylan was probably calling to complain about sales, promotion and accounting. That's what everybody called Clive about.

It was several years later, at a CBS party given just before the Firesign departed the label that Dylan and I almost met. Columbia had a new president — a forgettable accountant with abscessed advances and impacted residuals.

When we arrived at the affair, the word was out — "Dylan is definitely coming!" Shortly after, he appeared in our midst — small and familiar, with ten feet of open space around him.

I watched while the accountant, in his role as chief corporate executive, introduced Dylan to one of my comedian friends. A tiny peephole appeared in the protective barrier that such celebrities generate, the narrow eyes flicked up to the comedian's face, the peephole closed. The brief handclasp was ended. All the many things my friend had been saving up to say died unsaid.

A.J. Weberman, who was noted for his periodic raids on Dylan's garbage can, and who founded the "Dylan Archives" in Greenwich Village, wrote me a letter once. He wanted a free copy of the

Firesign's "Big Book of Plays" so he could write an article about our use of such symbols as "shoes" and "entrenching tools."

"I'm on to youse," Weberman wrote, "like I was on to Dylan." I found that a little scary and kept an eye out for strangers in my trash afterwards.

The Firesign was once employed to write a screenplay based on a highly surreal treatment of "Siddhartha," in which the hero was a Western gunfighter. The creator of this fantasy, one Joe Massot, intended the part to be played by Dylan. Good ol' Bob remarked (in a *Rolling Stone* interview), "I had a script a while ago that was called 'Zachariah and the Seven Cowboys.' (Laughs) That was some script. Every line in it was taken out of the Bible. And just thrown together."

The movie was made with John Rubinstein in Dylan's part, but that's another story entirely.

One of the best things about "Renaldo and Clara" was the appearance of Allen Ginsberg. What a delight to see his transformation from wild-haired guru to family doctor to Fairfax Avenue pensioner. What a great vaudeville team — Ginsberg and Dylan, the two great bardic singers of Our Time, discussing famous graves with each other! And Ginsberg reading "Kaddish" to ladies at a Catskill Mountains resort created the same sensations a whole circus full of acrobats might.

Thanks for the memories, Bob. Or are they only dreams?

THE THEME TODAY IS BOB (2007)

There's only a brief epilog to those non-encounters with Bob. Of course, everyone knows that he is elusive in the Heisenbergian range. If observed, you can bet the cat in the hat is dead, if you catch my metaphysical drift.

Bob played at the 2001 Grammys and we were there, in the immense and vacantly depressing negative space that advertises an office-supply chain and offers a lot of distant public seating with the sightlines of a nine-storey cruise ship. Bob was there on the stage. We were clustered with a motley crew of classical soloists, Apache drummers, yard-wide Rap Daddies and the guy that always wins the Polka Prize.

Bob was far away, in a big box, tight with his musicians, targeted by a couple of steadycamers, his back to us. That's where he played. He had that "Love and Theft" moustache then, but we couldn't see it. He was kinda All Hat. We loved it.

And the nominees are . . .

MICKEY'S BIRTHDAY PARTY

Mickey Mouse turned 50 last week and showed up at the White House after a cross-country train ride complete with whistle-stop appearances. Seldom in popular history is such a to-do made over the birthday of a fictitious character. (Only Sherlock Holmes and the collective William Shakespeare come to mind.) Mickey danced on network news with the President's daughter — something of a fictitious character herself. He even got sung to by J-I-M-M-Y. Why? Because we love good publicity!

Mickey, if you'll pardon me for saying so, was born with a silver screen in his mouth. Right from the opening of "Steamboat Willie" in Manhattan late in the great year of 1928 his success was assured. The Mouse went from two-dimensional cartoons to three-dimensional collectables in just a couple of years. By the time I was old enough to care what was printed on the bottom of my cereal bowl it was The Mouse. He became one of the household gods of the 20th century and virtually give birth to the idea of "merchandising."

I learned to read from the Disney comics, but soon hit the harder stuff (Superman and "Tales from the Crypt"). I still read the Mickey strip that appears in my weekly copy of Grit ("America's Greatest Family Newspaper"). In last week's, the Mouse was about to play a practical joke: "I'll pull the old squirting flower gag on Goofy!" says Mickey.

Goofy (what is Goofy anyway, a dog?) is watering his lawn. He turns around and sprays Mickey in the face (SPLASH). "Gawrsh! Sorry, Mickey!" (BLUB!) "It was an accident!" apologizes Goofy in his great dumb voice. Another fine moral lesson in six panels.

Mickey was a guest-star in the first movie I ever saw — "Fantasia." Buried in the lowest stratum of my movie memories, along with dying dinosaurs, flying horses and dancing alligators, is cheerful, determined Mickey — the plucky little every-mouse who loses control over his life (like the rest of us) and is literally overwhelmed by the results. Cheerful determination seems to be The Mouse's most notable attribute.

Like Bergen's Charlie McCarthy, Disney's Mickey Mouse was the "Boss's" alter-ego. No more a "real" mouse than Charlie was a real "boy," Mickey actually became corporate spokescreature for Disney Studios. Whereas L. B. Mayer, Harry Cohn and Jack Warner only had themselves, Walt had happy, generous, popular Mickey Mouse.

The little guy was a real Movie Star, too. No doubt of that. He kept company with the other Stars of the Thirties, won his Academy Awards, went off to war along with The Flag, Lucky Strikes and Coca-Cola. In the Fifties, everybody's stardom became suddenly insecure and Mickey became straight-man for Donald. He developed into a sort of semi-retired Bob Hope type who golfed. He was only 30 then, but acted 65.

At 50, the Mouse has survived even the Adult Backlash Effect — a phenomenon that put "mickey mouse" in the dictionary as "sentimental, insincere or characterized by trick effects." To say, "That's really mickey mouse!" used to be a sincere put-down. He was strictly for the kiddies fifteen years ago, before Walt's death and the great Disney nostalgia craze.

Interest in "Disneyana" has helped restore the Original Mouse to his status as a household idol. A publicity drawing released by the Studio shows the evolution of Three-Finger Mickey from simple sketch through a very dapper stage where he sported ears-in-perspective, to the most recent cuddly-bear look. But no matter what sort of would-be with-it clothing he dresses in, your Basic Mouse has a head made out of three circles. Remember, along with the Stars 'n' Stripes, The World with Mouse Ears flies high tonight over the Magic Kingdom.

I confess to having a few Mickey Mouse artifacts round my house, but I don't have a Mouse Phone. I might get a Donald Duck phone if he were available. The idea of hot-tempered Donald going "Wak! Wak! Wak!" and holding out the receiver seems more wonderful than taking it from a smiling black-and-white Original Mickey — who looks more than a little like those curbside "jockey boys" whose outstretched arms hold rings for horses instead of telephone customers. (There is a Snoopy phone — Mickey's only real competition for patron saint of merchandising is The Beagle — but I'm a cat person.)

Earlier this year, the AP ran a story about a collector and dealer of Mouse-iana who explained its appeal this way: "It's basic. Mickey's part of a very elementary morality system. Mickey is instantly recognizable and understandable. The colors and geometric relationships are perfect." The effects of The Mouse can actually be beneficial, like pyramids or crystals!

A recent ad for a $35 gold Mouse pendant ("authorized by Mickey's pals at the Walt Disney Studios") promises "Instant happiness for somebody wonderful. For you. Or for the Minnie Mouse in your life. Limit one pendant per order." That sounds suspiciously like a Blessed St. Mickey medal to me.

The topper to all this Mousellebration is the revelation that there is a real person under the out-size Mouse-head — a 20-year-old, 87-pound woman. That's all f-f-f-folks!

THE MOUSE HAS LEFT THE BUILDING (2007)

The Mouse is so yesterday! Now "Bugs!" They're something else. No, not the funny Bunny who sings opera and smooches Elmer Fudd. The Bugs in "my" Disney movie, "A Bugs Life."

Thanks to George Tirebiter, I landed an animation job, playing an elderly ant named Cornelius, in a movie that actually was Number One at the box office! My movie credits may be few, but they're groovy!

The studio recorded my voice on the old Disney lot in the same building where Pinto Colvig goofed on The Goof, Ducky Nash quacked, and the Main Street parade of Cliff Edwards, Robert Benchley, Sterling Holloway, Jerry Colonna, Edgar Bergen, Bing Crosby, Basil Rathbone and Ed Wynn lent their voices and characters to Disney's animators.

It seemed at the time as if little had changed at the corner of

Cinderella Street and Alice Avenue. Disney's dream was still a "campus" not a factory. It was a beautiful day, my director was Pixar's resident genius John Lasseter, and Roddy McDowall shared the waiting-room. I was scared to death.

By that time Mickey was nearly 75, far older than Walt had made it to, and probably spending most of his time, like Walt did, in Palm Springs. And while it's likely that Mickey Mouse will be around as long as Jee-zus H. Christ, his cinematic successor, that very unanimatronic Pirate of the Caribbean, little Johnny Depp, is sailing around the breakwater, bound for another billion bucks. Get in line now!

FUTURESHOCK IN A BOX

I stopped by a Lower State Street store the other day to buy a few batteries. I seldom drop into electronics stores — I have a lifelong distaste for wiring, instilled in me by an electric shop teacher at John Adams Junior High. A closet sadist, he would wire the classroom doorknob and wait for the first unsuspecting kid to come along, grab hold of it and yelp with the shock. He would also flail at us with a long metal rule, the other hand pressed against some dangerously open circuit. Sparks flew at us from the ruler's tip. All that gave me the impression that electricity was pretty weird and I never really buckled down to making the big project — a crystal set.

As I waited for the business of buying batteries to conclude, my nervous fascination with The Future drew me toward a display featuring the store's sample home computer. Amazing! More amazing even than a wire-it-yourself smoke alarm with solar-powered 8-track!

This, I thought, is IT! The robot house that Ray Bradbury dreamt of back in the Fifties while strolling through the City by night, seeing the green auras of the Big Tube through every front window — the robot house that vacuums itself, serves you breakfast and entertains the kids — is now a practical reality. Here, starting at $559, is its bionic brain — a TV screen, a typewriter keyboard and a portable cassette!

A plug for this unit in a magazine called *Creative Computing* says it's "idiot-proof" — which probably means that the folks down at Creative Computing don't subscribe to the old theory that an unlimited number of monkeys poking away at an equal number of typewriters will eventually write *War and Peace*. I don't either. An unlimited number of me's poking away at that computer keyboard would never come up with the Secret of the Universe — not unless they learn to speak BASIC. That spells Beginner's All-Purpose Symbolic Instruction Code (actually that spells BAPSIC, but the ways of computer acronyms are mysterious! A knowledge of BASIC — or BAPSIC — will allow you to ask your little Household Hal such questions as "Why am I overdrawn at the bank?" or "What is my social security number?" or "Help! My computer's gone berserk!" as well as to string limited variables all day if you want to.

This machine does seem to be more than just an expensive way to balance your taxes, remember your phone numbers and give you the time and temp in downtown Tokyo. Its interchangeable parts bring it out of the office and into the heart of the home. It seems destined to involve the Whole Family, just as the Tube did thirty years ago.

If you're not satisfied with your microwave food-zapper, already programmed to fix dinner faster than you can earn the money to pay for it, you can hook it up to the computer's Home Recipe Program. As the company blurb says, "It won't take long before you'll wonder how you ever worked in the kitchen without your computer!" And while you're wondering, you can convert pints into liters, dollars to donuts and all the ingredients in Uncle Absenth's quiche recipe, so you'll know how many eggs you'll need to serve Fifty Million Frenchmen. It may even be able to do the impossible — add oranges and apples.

By shoving another $5 cassette into the machine's maw, you can play what the booklet calls "time-honored games" — blackjack and backgammon. "Great fun for parties," they say, "at the office or at home after an exhausting day." Imagine Joe Looser coming home from an exhausting day at the office where they've been playing cutthroat backgammon with the petty cash since the boss left for Hawaii. He ignores the wife, cracks a can of Bud, sits down in front of the old Video Display, admires his Expansion Options and Peripherals, snaps in the latest software and loses hand after hand of blackjack while little Hal consoles him by pointing out, "Tough luck, Bozo, you lose again" over and over.

No, seriously folks — I love my computer. Instead of "Starsky & Hutch" I watch Descriptive Statistics, Simple Correlations and Linear Regression. There's not a lot of difference, you know? I mean, why bother with "Lou Grant" when I have my own Editor/Assembler Program with Standard Silog mnemonics? My only regret is the macros and conditional assemblies are not supported. But what is, these days?

Little Electra — she's nine years old Saturday and up to Chapter 4 already and doing very well. Darlene — that's the little woman — she's only up to Chapter 3, but that's because Little Buddy hogs the set playing Star Wars 2001 every day when he comes home from Social Orientation.

Now that's Total Versatility, just like the book says.

I could actually be writing this very copy down on a computer at my desk, editing and correcting as I go along. I could DELETE the rest of the line and insert string. POKE your GOTO and INPUT your CLOAD — this is DIM END ERROR! REST, RESTORE and RESUME! GET PUT and KILL RESET! Look out for those dummy parameters and don't forget to RANDOMIZE the LSET.

If this is programming, I say, make the most of it.

My futureshock fantasy concluded along with the business of battery-buying. I also now owned a carbon copy of my receipt, with my own name and address and phone number on it. Handwritten. Twice, because the clerk first made a calculating error on the mechanical cash register.

Good old manpower, combined with human error, had triumphed again. And that's something we all can understand.

WAITER, THERE'S A PHONE IN MY SHOE! (2007)

OK, so you can chat while you vedge, game while you Google, surf while you snap and let everyone in the world see you fall on your ass, back your van into your mother-in-law, shave your unmentionables and send you and Big Ben blogging home to Bangkok in the blink of a megabite. Sorry, not my thing.

But this here ancient Mac I'm writing on, preserved since the Gay Nineties, is doing its job — no carbons. That's a bit of awrite! Because writing, Dear Friends, is rewriting. The computer does make it easier. Research a click or two away, Drafts preserved in cybercode. E-mail off to my publisher. That back-space turned "delete" works real well.

But that's it, dearly beloved! I like my screens Wide. I despise the sound of some random pop song breaking out two rows away in the darkness of my local playhouse. Puleeeze don't show me what instantly happened, I can wait for tomorrow's *Times*. And the very idea of watching more about yesterday's TV shows on my telephone is more than futureshock. It's the triumph of meaninglessness, the unwanted gift of "content providers" to a society that's lost its collective sense of touch.

Excuse me, I have to get that . . .

UFOVERDOSE

"There's a Seeker born every minute!
Dr. "Happy" Harry Cox, UFOlogist

Floodlights suspended in the darkness over the arena gleam like UFOs. A violet glow pulses up from the parking lot behind Santa Barbara's Horse Showgrounds. Komar the Firewalker, a 44-portly in brown tweed and white espadrilles, is drinking a can of Coke, preparing for his stroll through a pit of coals, now cooling off visibly in the chilly California evening.

It's Friday, opening night of the Clearlight Energy Conference — a $70 weekend advertising "The most complete assemblage of International Teachers of New Age Wisdom and Knowledge ever brought together in our time!" We're all ready, but the New Age is running a couple of hours late.

Several people stand around the arena wearing golden wire pyramids for hats. They are very serious about this, even the girl whose pyramid is modishly denim-covered. A miniature film crew readies their Super-8s under the direction of an Old Hollywood Hand in a cream leisure suit who seems all ready for "It Happened One Night."

Komar takes off his loafers and socks, rolls up his pants, strides barefooted to the edge of the coals, takes a big drag from his Marlboro and a long pull from a fresh Coke. The coals look hotter now that the red spotlights have been turned on.

It takes ten minutes for Komar to go into a sugar-and-nicotine trance. Then he raises his hand and paces deliberately down the middle of the 20-foot pit. It takes only a few seconds. The audience applauds and Komar smiles faintly. His feet are bright pink and still have a few embers stuck to them. We crowd around the coals to look at his footprints and stay to keep warm.

Inside the neighboring auditorium, the Con is being MC'd by Rennie Davis, once a Chicago Seven activist who comes on now with Orphan Annie eyes, a perpetual off-center smile and an extensive wardrobe. It's a disappointingly small crowd, made larger by a heaping ashram-ful of Maharaj-Ji devotees, a full rock 'n' roll sound and light crew and what seem to be a lot of freebies, like me.

Sales tables edge the auditorium. Pyramid hats are a popular item, along with Egyptian Power Posters, negative ion generators and flying saucer postcards. It's no surprise that most of the Con speakers have lines of products and services available. ("We make no claims, but our results are 100%!") There's a medicine show air about these fellows in polyester turtlenecks, gold power amulets and shiny shoes.

We're listening to pyramidologist Bill Cox, who advises us to eat with our eyes closed. All this is not a fad, he says, "but a speeding wave engulfing the planet."

Uri Geller's California competition, a zippy former ad man named Lawrence Kennedy, shows us slides of twisted cutlery, knotted fireplace tools and his teenaged son purportedly bending whole kitchens worth of pots and pans. Kennedy demonstrates a feat Geller "won't perform." He holds two spoons in his out-stretched hands and strokes the handles with his thumbs. Both spoons develop a small bend as we watch. The house gives him a modest hand. We are not convinced.

"Now," he says, "work on your own spoons." His pointy-hatted helpers pass out a carton of thrift-shop flatware. Lots of folks around me stroke their handles. "You've got to really make physical love to that spoon," he urges.

"I did it!" exclaims a young lady in front of me. She holds out her doubled-up spoon. Soon, similar reactions from a half-dozen people in my area. The energy radiates and at last the Con-goers seem to have gotten what they came for.

Saturday morning, the Docs come down to give us the sacred word. Dr. Marcel Vogel, whose inventions have made IBM rich, now talks with plants ("I owe my being with you today to the greatest teacher I ever had — a split-leaf philodendron") and believes he can develop a videotape thought recorder.

He's followed by Dr. Ray Brown, a burly ex-scuba diver who brings with him a fist-sized crystal ball which he tells us he discovered in an underwater pyramid in the Bermuda Triangle. This fabulous find turned him from treasure-hunter to holistic healer. "We're reviving the aura of homeopathy and giving it the New Age Image," he tells us.

Then Dr. Frank Dorland entertains with gorgeous photos of the famous crystal "Skull of Doom." This ancient artifact, found in Mexico in 1926 . . .

But continuity is interrupted by the follow next to me who claims to be an Emergency Room MD and reggae producer from Arizona. He proffers a baggie of Rainbow Light Mushrooms. Naturally organic.

Onstage, a grandmotherly Brazilian attempts to discuss "extra-cerebral memory." I am having great trouble following her use of personal pronouns. The Doc and I have more mushrooms. The Brazilian describes her "spiritual tunaboat" and "out-of-bed" experiences. I take one little mushroom for later and flee the Con.

Everything has gone all cosmic mellow by the time I return. The devotees are singing "Save me from this material world," and doing an Isadora-style interpretive dance, while an electrified musician plays "Gas Music From Arcturus" on his blue violin.

A man from NASA gives up a slide show about the Space Shuttle. He's very young and refers to the 1969 Moon Landing as "the one you remember." This is Bozo stuff. He doesn't realize he's got a room full of folks who shuttle through Space in their sleep.

Rennie Davis, in evening clothes, brings on the headliner, Rev. Robert Short, a short red-haired, white-suited man with an open channel to the Solar Presidium. He predicts, possessed of an alien voice with a faint burr, like "Enterprise" Engineer Scott, "the final round and countdown to the destruction of civilization." I hurry outside to look for the expected Close Encounter. The only thing that looks like a UFO is the auditorium building itself. I take off. The building doesn't.

Sunday, the Con is on again. I ask Rennie Davis if he's bothered that none of the speakers seem to mention practical, worldly applications of their psychic discoveries to urgent social needs, like zapping the internal combustion engine. He's not. "This conference should inspire us all to turn inward, stay out of the way and surrender to God." The idea of a cluster of mighty golden pyramids under the hood of a Dodge doesn't interest him much.

As the final speakers talk about the astral plane ("where you can dress like Napoleon and you are Napoleon") and mind control ("think of yourself as gods and nothing is impossible"), one of the Clearlight people draws me aside to reveal some startling news. "The Conference is a success!" he confides. "The camera crew hasn't had to change batteries in three days! As a matter of fact they were over-charged this morning!"

They weren't the only ones. (1978)

BROTHER BILL vs. BEAT ST. JACK
Editorial Counterpoints

ROLL THE ORGAN & CANARIES MUSIC CUE

Hello, Dear Friends, this is Brother Bill Barnstormer, founder of the Old Established Church of Science, Fiction. Oh, we hear a lot these troubled days about Patriotism. Say Thank You for that! But what must we do NOW to prove ourselves a grateful nation unto the Admistration? How can we say Thank You to the Leadership Committee of the U.S.? I know you've wrapped your car in the Flag of our Homeland and glued the "Don't Tread on U.S." sticker on the window behind the gunrack. And They know too — the Admistration knows because even though they got those satellite photos of your truck or SUV they didn't target your butt, and you can say Thank You for that!

You say the Pledge of Allegiance, in the Revised Standard version, before breakfast and important business and social meetings. Thank You!

You identify yourself completely with the rigid and authoritarian hierarchy of the military-industrial complex. Yes!

You mingle your local church, synagogue or mosque as deeply as you can into the politics of fundamental rights and freedoms. That's right!

In every word and deed you support the right of some unelected human beings to triumphulate

over others and you vote NO on school and
rapid transit bonds. You know that nothing
is "a matter of opinion" and you pray — say
Thank You — for affirmative answers to what
you think is right already. Yes!

And still, many of us simply can't be
Patriotic enough, we can't thank our
Internal and International Security Forces
enough, but most of all, what can we say to Him?

"Dear Friends, let him hear you love him,
that's all. Write a letter to Him at the
White House in Washington, D.C. and say,

Mr. President, I love you and I feel good
now, like you said you did after you started
Your War, and I feel prideful and important
and full of brass tacks, just like you do,
Sir. And I say Thank you, because I know —
Freedom is a Bush on Fire! Give us a light,
and we'll follow him anywhere! Thank You.
This is Brother Bill Barnstormer

ROLL TITLE: BILL UNDERMUTTER'S "REALITY" UPDATE

NASTY MUSIC UNDER:

"As they hunker down for combat in the coming
television season, the major network rivals
are promising several snazzy 'reality' series
new this fall: On PBS, 'Graverobbers'
Roadshow Abroad' broadcasts from several
Middle East bazaars, including surprising
finds in Old Bagdad! CBS offers 'I Live in
My Cadillac' with has-been host Georgie
Tirebiter parked under the Hollywood Freeway,
and NBC gives you 'My Worst Nightmare' as
underage celebrities struggle to keep jobs
they know nothing about, like atomic-plant
maintenance and German auto repair."

NEWS THEME MUSIC IN UNDER

"Finally, HBO leaves not a lot to the imagination
on 'The Pit and the Pendulum,' based on the
S. and M. Poe classic, featuring premature
burial, sexy vampires and lots of rats! This
is Bill Undermutter for CNNo Evil News, all
over the Imperium. . . . Coming up, more of
the same with subtitles."

MUSIC OUT

BEAT ST. JACK'S
BLACK HAWK CELL-PHONE NIGHTMARE

[Thank you and gimme some trance-mix.... Yeah... Ooo... Click here now!]

TRANCE MIX IN AND UNDER

You can read while you chat while you vedge while you phone
while you eat 'cause you can from a can on the can in your van
on the lam
from the Black Hawks overhead in your head.

Get a grip, it's your trip, you can game while you smile
while you colon close parentheses smile,
watch DVDs
in your BVD's
7-24 on-line takeout in a 7-11 neon heaven
you're right at home where the Smiling Slushy Guy
who helps on the fly
takes out each Black Hawk that's landin' in your head

Listen in, your phone is ringin' Dragnet, it's ringin' Star Wars,
it's ringin' 8 Mile, listen Sk8erBoi, it's downloadin'
your stock market investment portfolio Happy Funds Account
while you freekin' vedge!
While you duck the sneaky feeling
you're a gamer loser gamer over under heavy fire from the
Black Hawks still circlin' in your head.

Hey, you can still sing karaoke with some Okie if you want to
from Okefenokee to Old Smokey
on the little color screen
big as the boxes of matches you don't carry,
'cause you're not smokin' like you used to, no, sir,
you're drinkin' Fiji water
and jokin' on the phone to Joan, you know it's Joan
'cause there's her picture, bright as a two-billion-year-old galaxy,

clear as Midnight on the Tigris,
there on the little screen,
on the foldable phone
that rings and rings like a man in a music-box
and rings all night like a sax singin' in a subway
where you dream you're joggin' in your Vicky underwear
under where the Black Hawks keep stalkin'
the last pockets
of resistance
in the wireless wonderworld
of your post-war
pomme-de-terre.

DO and Phil Austin, "Radio Team"

Part Five

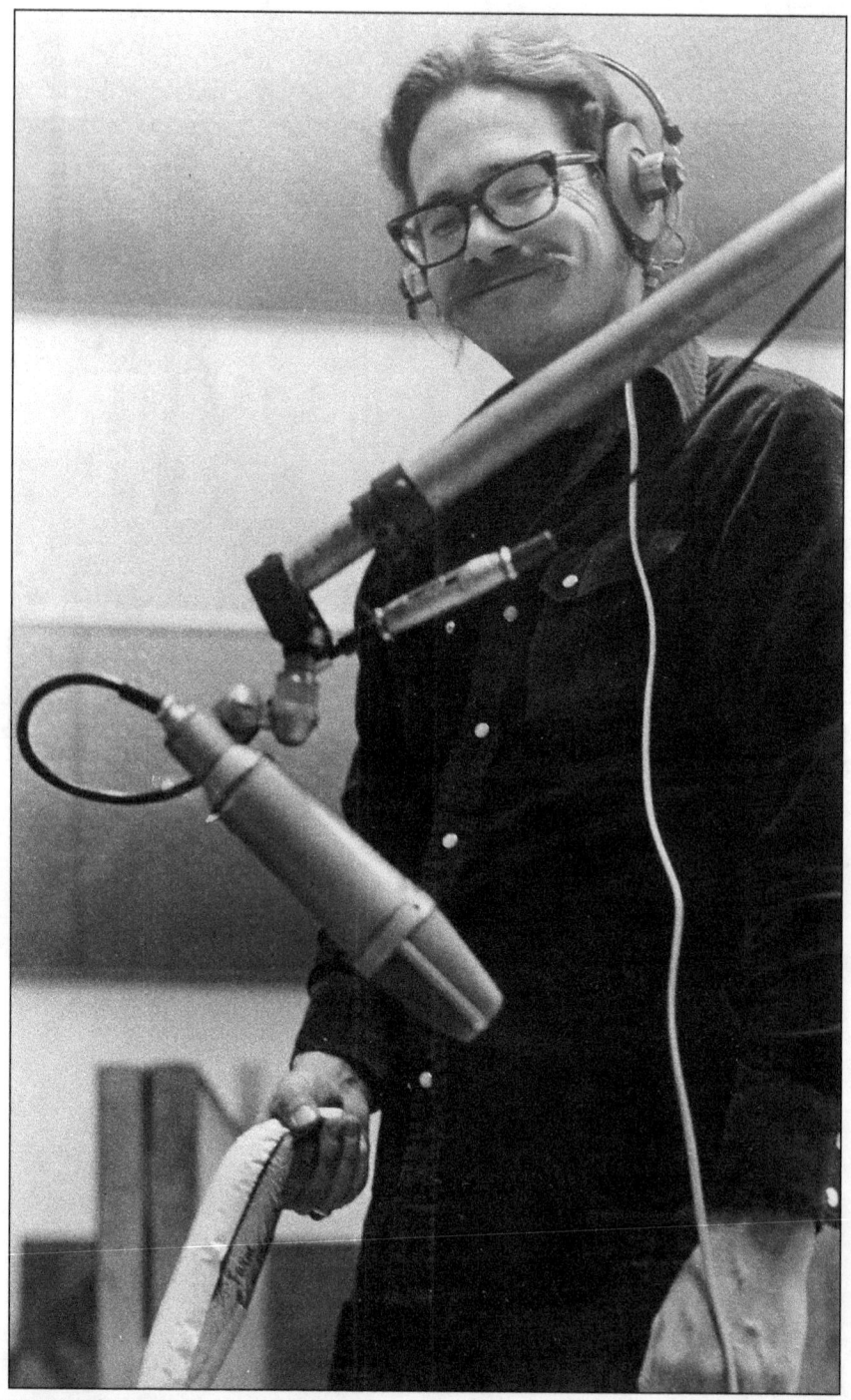

"A Satisfying Foley Sound Effect"

Fun with Radio Theatre

COMEDY, MYSTERY, SCI-FI, SCRIPTS AND TIPS

1. "WHEN I'M ON THE RADIO WITH YOU" . . . 177
    GEORGE TIREBITER'S RADIO THEME SONG

2. A "GOLDEN AGE" RADIO DOUBLE-BILL . . . 178
    TWO OF TIREBITER'S (AND OSSMAN'S) FAVORITE ROLES:
    "WHO'S PEGGY?"
    A WORK-OUT FOR RADIO SOUNDMAN AND FALSETTO
    "MAX MORGAN, CRIME CABBY"
    A HARD-BOILED POEM FOR RADIO

3. RADIO: SPACE, TIME AND MIND . . . 202
    THE POWER OF THE MEDIUM.
    MY FAVORITE MONSTER (1978)
    LOOK NO FURTHER THAN THE WAR OF THE WORLDS.
    W.O.W.! (1988)
    A DIRECTOR'S COMMENTS ON THE 50TH-ANNIVERSARY PRODUCTION.
    SCIENCE FICTION AND THE THEATRE OF THE MIND (2006)
    SOME PERSONAL HISTORY ON THE POPULAR GENRE.

4. "THE FUTURE RADIO ADVENTURES OF MARK TIME" . . . 212
    THE COMMANDER AND HIS PALS DOC TECHNICAL AND BOB BUNNY, HARASSED BY THEIR MALFUNCTIONING ROSCO ROBOT, GO ON A SPYING MISSION TO A CERTAIN FUEL-RICH MIDDLE EASTERN PLANET X.
    SCRIPTS FOR FIRESIGN'S XM SERIES "FOOLS IN SPACE." (2001)

5. A RADIO THEATRE PRIMER . . . 241
    NICK'S FIRST RULE: KEEP YOUR THUMB NEXT TO YOUR LINE, SO YOU WON'T LOSE YOUR PLACE IN THE SCRIPT! (1996)

6. THE GEORGE TIREBITER MYSTERY . . . 247
    "THE DOOR THAT IS ALWAYS OPEN AND CLOSED"
    THE PILOT EPISODE, TO BE CONTINUED. (2002)

DO and Judith Walcutt, Live From the Islands, KSER, 2003

"WHEN I'M ON THE RADIO WITH YOU"
As Sung by Frank Funnk & Margot Mundaigne in George Tirebiter's Radio Follies

Words by David Ossman Music by Rick Ingrasci

Even if you can't tell De Forest from de tree,
When you stand in front of a microphone with me,
Coast-to-coast our hook-up is,
But somehow we don't care –
Hand-in-hand we steal a kiss
Before we're "On The Air" . . .

Being on the radio with you,
A million listeners hear us bill and coo.
When I gently whisper "I love you" in your ear –
A lady in Sheboygan turns the volume UP TO HEAR!
For everything we say
Is broadcast far away,
When I'm on the radio with you.

When they turn those kilocycles on,
Darling, all our privacy is gone.
And if we should indulge in a single naughty word
A gentleman from Uncle Sam 'akes 'ure it 'on't be 'heard!
He 'on't 'eave us alone,
Behind the 'icrophone,
When I'm on the radio with you
For everything we say
Is broadcast far away,
When I'm on the radio with you!

A "GOLDEN AGE" DOUBLE-BILL
"WHO'S PEGGY?"
A Work-Out for Soundman and Falsetto
&
MAXWELL MORGAN, CRIME CABBY
A Hard-Boiled Poem for Radio

Here are two of my favorite roles: First, the falsetto joy of "Peggy," the heroine of the soap-opera "Who's Peggy?" "Peggy" has been reincarnated in one desperate situation or another ("Over the Edge" is her other series) for years on various stages. Tirebiter originally created the character when he had to substitute unexpectedly for a missing actress — his wife!

Then, hard-driving, hard-drinking, hyperbolic "Max Morgan," the *noir* cabby-poet, written in language patterned after the high-toned "literary" style of the better pulp and radio hacks. And a "hack" is just what Max drives! A few more notes about the production of the audio play follow the text.

"WHO'S PEGGY?"
PHOTO BY PATRICIA PENCE

"WHO'S PEGGY?"

As performed by Phil Proctor, Loren Churchill and David Ossman in "George Tirebiter's Radio Follies"

ANNOUNCER (PHIL): AAAcme Brothers, makers of Glamorama Hand and Body Bar, and Dead Cat Soap — "The Washday Wonder" — present . . .

MUSIC: THEME IN HARD AND UNDER

ANN: "WHO'S PEGGY?" . . . the sobering story of Peggy, and who the average housewife feels when she must find out for herself the little things that her husband does not know, and face the fact that life goes on — even — over the edge . . .

MUSIC: THEME SURGES, THEN INTO BG

ANN: But first — girls, you know germs are Nature's worst enemies! And everyday germs can be the most dangerous! That's why Glamorama Hand and Body Bar is 96.7 percent germ-free. Its secret cleaning agents say "boo" to nasty germs wherever they may be — on your hands, in your dirty clothing, or all over the little ones. So, to avoid colds, flu, or (SNEEZES) even worse — buy and always use disease-fighting Glamorama Soap — it's double purified. Look for the Hollywood Starlet on every bar. And now . . .

MUSIC: THEME SURGES, THEN UNDER

SOUND: INCLUDES KNITTING, BIRDS SINGING, SHEARS OUTSIDE, AND THEN, WITH THE NARRATION, A CLAP OF THUNDER, RAIN AND A KNOCK ON THE DOOR.

ANN: As you may remember from day-before-yesterday, it's still a still Thursday afternoon in early spring. Peggy sits by her sitting-room window, knitting, waiting for her desperate husband, Random. Outside, the monotonous chatter of hedge shears is drowned out by the monotonous patter of a sudden storm. Peggy isn't expecting the unexpected knock at the front door.

SOUND: KNOCK

MUSIC: FADES OUT UNDER

GLT (AS PEGGY): (HUMMING AS SHE KNITS, THEN) Who is it?

PHIL (OFF, AS YANK): Yank Knob, Miz Peggy!

PEGGY: Why — do come in, Yank . . .

SOUND: DOOR OPENS, RAIN COMES UP

YANK: Yer greens 're as trim as Hitler's moustache, Miz Pee! I woulda got them owls out from under the porch, too, if the rains hadn'ta started up.

PEGGY: Come all the way in, Yank, and — close the door.

SOUND: DOOR CLOSES

YANK: How's that?

PEGGY: Fine . . . you . . you must be — wet . . .

YANK: I'll just slip outta my boots right here, Miz Pee.

SOUND: EACH BOOT DROPPED TO FLOOR

PEGGY: I certainly admire a man with big — feet, Yank. Why not — make us a cool drink?

PHIL: Well, yeah — why sure, I . . .

PEGGY: Lemonade and ice and — gin — right over here — in the window seat, Yank . . . See?

SOUND: SHE WALKS ACROSS THE FLOOR IN HEELS AND OPENS THE SQUEAKY TOP OF THE WINDOW SEAT. YANK WALKS BAREFOOTED ACROSS THE FLOOR

PEGGY: Such — strong feet, too . . . Yes, that's it, Yank . . .

SOUND: YANK PUTS ICE INTO A PAIR OF GLASSES, POURS DRINKS

YANK: Is this all right, Miz Pee?

PEGGY: You don't need to call me "Miz," you know, Yank. I'm not — your Mother . . .

YANK: But — you're — you're like her, uh, Peggy . . .

PEGGY: Cheers!

SOUND: CLINKING TWO GLASSES

PEGGY: Just — how am I like — your Mother . . . ?

YANK: Well, yer dressed purty much the same . . . that's a flimsy burnoose, ain't it?

PEGGY: It certainly is . . .

YANK: And, well, the fillin's purty much the same — uh — shape . . .

PEGGY: (DRINKING) Oh! Yank, I . . . I'm so glad you think so. I . . .

YANK: Peggy, er, gosh . . .

PEGGY: Oh, Yank! (A CLINCH, PASSIONATELY KISSING BACKS OF HANDS) Mmmmmmm . . . (BREAKING AWAY) Oh, no — no — Yank! My husband, Random, he — he might be coming home any minute, and . . .

YANK: That means we've got to hurry!

PEGGY: Oh, no, Yank! Let me . . . Oh! (THEY CLINCH AGAIN) . . . Go! That's his car pulling into the driveway now!

SOUND: HIGH POWERED CAR PULLING IN WITH A SCREECH

YANK: I guess I could just — go back outside . . .

PEGGY: No! You've got to hide! Oh! Quickly — get into the window-seat!

YANK: But Miz Pee . . .

PEGGY: Get in!

SOUND: YANK CLIMBING IN AND BEING PUSHED DOWN. THEN SQUEAKY LID OF SEAT SLAMMED SHUT.

YANK: I . . . Uhphhhh . . . wait . . .

PEGGY: Oh! You look just like Cary Grant in "Arsenic and Old Lace!"

YANK: (INSIDE) Mrrrrrummphhh . . .

PEGGY: There now. Random just comes home to have a cigarette and a highball and talk about work, and then he goes right back to the penitentiary. Oh! Yank! Your boots!

SOUND: SHE RUNS IN HER MULES ACROSS THE ROOM, OPENS THE SQUEAKY LID, THROWS THE BOOTS IN ON TOP OF YANK.

YANK: (SUDDENLY UNMUFFLED) I could just leave now an' come back an' git them owls later . . .

SOUND: LID SLAMMED SHUT

YANK: (INSIDE) Mmmmmmmrrrrrrrphhh . . .

PEGGY: Shhhh! I'll just sit right here — on top of — everything . . .

SOUND: DOOR OPENS, BURST OF RAIN, RANDOM'S HEAVY FOOTSTEPS WITH AN ACCOMPANYING JANGLE, AS IF HEAVY KEYS, HANDCUFFS, ETC., COMING ON

PEGGY: Why, Random! What a sweet surprise! No! Don't say a word! Come, kiss me first!

SOUND: RANDOM CROSSES. THEY KISS.

PEGGY: (BREAKING AWAY) Have a drink, Random. I already made it for you, see? There it is . . . By your favorite chair. Just relax . . .

SOUND: RANDOM SLURPING DRINK

PEGGY: That's it . . . No, dear. Please! Don't tell me how bad you feel. I just won't listen. Why don't you — turn on the radio, Random . . .

SOUND: HIS FOOTSTEPS AND JANGLE GO OFF, CLICK OF RADIO ON

MUSIC: AS IF ON THE RADIO, VERY SOTTO ROMANTIC DANCE NUMBER

PEGGY: That's better, don't you think? Oh, I know you do. Is it raining hard downtown? Effie Shoe called to say it was near to flooding down on Elm Street near the drugstore, so I know it is . . Ahh . . . would you like a cigarette, Random? Of course you would . . .

SOUND: CELLOPHANE OF CIGARETTE PACKAGE, TAMPING OUT

PEGGY: And — a light . . . ?

SOUND: MATCH STRIKES AND FLARES

PEGGY: Oh, Random — when you're so close — like this — I — I — ohh . . . (THEY CLINCH) Random! Your lips are so cruel! I — wait!. . .No! Stay away from the window-seat! Random!

SOUND: HIS FOOTSTEPS JANGLE ACROSS ROOM. TOP OF SEAT FLUNG BACK. CRASH OF BOTTLES AND GLASSES.

YANK: Gosh! Hello, sir. I can explain everything — I . . .

SOUND: A PISTOL SHOT, TERRIBLE CRASH OF GLASS AND BODY FALL

PEGGY: SCREAMS

MUSIC: INTO THEME HARD AND THEN UNDER

ANN: Stay tuned again tomorrow, as everyone asks the question . . . "Who's Peggy?" "Who's Peggy?" is written and created by Visalia Bakersfield, from the best-selling novel "The Ambushed Heart," by Selma Owens Lake. Lillie LaMonte is usually heard as Peggy, with Blythe Barstow and Eureka Fillmore as The Twins, Julian Brawley as Random, Willits Lodi as Tricky, Petaluma Gilroy as Gramps, Irvine S. Condido as George Spoon and Modesto Livermore as Yank. Today's episode directed by Dinuba Turlock. This is Reedly L. Centro speaking. . .

MUSIC: THEME UP AND OUT

George Tirebiter as "Maxwell Morgan"

MAXWELL MORGAN — CRIME CABBY
A HARD-BOILED POEM FOR RADIO

CAST
ANNOUNCER A warm, deep male voice of authority.

ANNOUNCER 2 A genuinely sexy female narrator.

FERGUS A day-shift bartender, talkative, unfulfilled. Series regular and Max's comic foil.

MAX MORGAN A Los Angeles cabdriver who gets involved in a weekly mystery on this series. Hard-boiled, yet poetic, in the style of the early 1950s.

RICK Piano bar pianist. No speaking lines. Comments musically as the story develops.

SALVADOR CUGAT Spokesman for cigar company sponsor. Interesting Latino accent.

CAPTAIN GROGAN Tough cop. Max's series nemesis.

MR. EASY Max's woman friend and a series regular. Mae West-ish delivery style.

MUSIC: Except for the scene in the police station, this play is underscored throughout with pre-1950 tunes, vamps and improvisations in the style of a piano-bar pianist. The music should be witty and conversational. The show's theme is the 1945 tune "Laura," by David Raksin.

SOUND: During the scenes in the bar, there is constant business associated with the washing and arrangement of glasses. There is also specific pouring-drink business. Fist-fights, blows to the head and warm kisses are heard in every episode. All sound should be Foley (live effects to match the action). No recorded effects should be heard in this show.

MAXWELL MORGAN — CRIME CABBY
"The Twin Trunk Affair"
(March 4, 1950)

ANNOUNCER: S. Pudd & Sons, makers of fine rolled-up tobacco products since World War One, invites you to "lay back, light one up," and enjoy a satisfying show — as DREAMO CIGARS presents MAXWELL MORGAN — CRIME CABBY . . .

MUSIC: PIANO BAR PIANO WITH THEME — "LAURA"

ANNOUNCER 2: It's another rain-soaked Friday night at the Doom Room — one of those quiet little shanties on the Malibu Coastline where a fella can finally rest his eyes from the hot glare of passing headlights. The joint's got a piano-bar shaped like a .45, lots of nets draped over the walls, and a big fish-tank full of mermaids. Just the right kind of atmosphere for the likes of a bruised and battered Maxwell Morgan . . .

MUSIC: CONTINUES UNDERSCORE THROUGHOUT, IMPROV

FERGUS: Max! Max Morgan! Come on in! Siddown! Say! You look like you had to eat one too many knuckle-burgers!

MAX: (SIGHS) Gimme a double-shot of the hard sauce and hold the wise-acres, Fergus. Life is a tough case and another two-bit fare nearly closed the book on mine.

SOUND: BAR NOISES AD LIB THROUGHOUT.

FERGUS: (POURING) Don't you ever pick up no

old ladies on a joy-ride up to Glendale?
Some Hollywood glamour-babe, out for a swell
time in the backseat on some back street?

MAX: I gotta say, it's a checkered business,
Fergus.

FERGUS: I know ya ain't yellow, Max.

MUSIC: SLIDES INTO SOMETHING UP-BEAT

MAX: Hold it, Rick, you ivory-mangler! Play
me somethin' low down and dirty, friend.
(DRINKS) Ah! Slide that rye on down the
bar . . . yeah . . .

MUSIC: SEGUES BACK TO BLUES

SOUND: BOTTLE SLIDES, CLINK OF GLASS, POURS

MAX: I'll tell ya how I picked up the nicks on
this ugly mug . . . (DRINKS) Ah! Well, it's
been comin' down like wet lead slugs since
early this afternoon, right? I was cruisin'
Wilshire Boulevard — you know, stoppin' at
every corner for the red light and checkin'
out the "latest styles," looking for a nice
quiet run up Coldwater — maybe over to the
Valley — dollar tip and chicken dinner at the
Ol' Plantation House — when all-of-a-sudden
this elderly gent with a mug like a goat
toddles out from under an awning, gives me a
hail, and jumps in Ol' Betsy like a scared
turkey cobbler.

FERGUS: He musta seen yer smilin' beezer
through the wind-shield and thought you was
his guardian angel.

MAX: Nope! He's got his head too far inside the 9-Star Final to gimme a peep. I sez, "OK, buddy, where to?" And he sez: "Santa Monica Sanitarium, Butch, and make it snappy!" Which is pretty salty for an old bird, but I high-tail it into the sunset. If there was a sunset . . .

FERGUS: I know that lay-out. Word's out it's a hide-out for fat-cats.

MAX: Sure. Over-weight oilmen, a couple of generals who'll drink anything with three stars on it, your local Congressman on the run from some Washington Widow. I got a regular fare uses the joint when he "owes too much on his insurance policy."

FERGUS: I always wanted to work in a place like that — chrome cocktail shakers, a swell parade of bonded hooch marchin' past the cut-glass mirrors back of the bar, war reports on the Philco, and a stock-tickler in the steam-room . . .

MAX: I drop the Ol' Skeezix off at the front stoop, and he tells me, "Keep yer flag down!" The rain on the roof and the meter tickin' make a nice racket. I'm in no hurry, so I pull out a smoke and read a few jokes in the Digest . . .

FERGUS: "Life in These United States?"

MAX: Sure. And "Humor in Uniform."

BOTH: "It Pays to Increase Your Word Power."

MAX: Yeah! Serendipitous. Well, pretty soon the geezer comes back haulin' a steamer trunk as big as Union Station. I sez, "No chance in Hades, brother!" He's pushin' and shovin' at the thing to get it inta the back seat. Well, it's as heavy as a stevedore's mother-in-law, but I help him wrestle it in. He tells me I should hustle it out to one o' them Big Businessman's Beach Clubs down on the Highway. Drive around back and unload it by the service door. Then he hands me a double-sawbuck and hot-foots it into the palm trees.

FERGUS: I used to tend bar, special, down to those beach places sometimes. Guys in double-breasted Packards and big Tuxedo convertibles. Downtown guys, with City Hall written all over their faces, like a neon beer sign. That's where they count the votes, alright — like handfuls of Havanas. The Jeremiah Club . . .

MAX: You called it for me, Fergus. Marble chandeliers and Oriental upholstery for the big-wigs out front, and a kitchen fulla Tia Juana tea-heads on the run from the Border Patrol. One of the "help" was out back on the sea-landin' when I got there — scrapin' fish-heads in the rain, and singin' some song about a Tropical Nightmare . . .

MUSIC: SWINGS INTO A LATIN NUMBER

FERGUS: Wow! That's a Bing Crosby song — "Tropical Nightmare."

MUSIC: SEGUES TO UNDERSCORE FIGHT WITH HARD CHORDS

MAX: Yeah? Well, look out, 'cause that's just what this Latin loafer turned out to be. I get out of the cab, quick — like always — and he's at me like a killer shark with the toothache!

SOUND: THE TWO MEN FIGHTING

MAX: (STRUGGLING) I've as good as got him . . . under control . . . when . . . I guess I slip on a fish-head and — whack!

SOUND: WHACK!

MAX: (CLUBBED AND FADING) My skull connects with a hard, flat thing I think is the wet asphalt pavement of the parking lot, but turns out to be a bolt of greasy lightning that knocks me off a high wall into a deep, wet place that covers me up tight under a blue-black blanket of blankness . . .

MUSIC: UP AND WITH POUNDING CHORDS, OUT.

ANNOUNCER: We'll return for Act Two of MAXWELL MORGAN — CRIME CABBY — after these words for DREAMO CIGARS from famous Surrealist Bandleader Salvador Cugat . . .

MUSIC: LATIN THEME UNDER

SALVADOR: Men! Stop envying those big, black Cuban cigars that make your favorite smoke look like a dead man's finger! Now — DREAMO CIGARS — the "First choice of men with a nickel to spend" — are proud to introduce DREAMO NEGROS! A surprisingly big cigar — made bigger with plenty of

rich, dark, heavily-veined Havana wrapper
— moist, meaty filler — and attractive,
pre-drilled tip that the ladies love! Look
for three Super Straight styles — Primo,
Perfecto and El Maximo! For men with more
on their minds than just action! DREAMO
NEGROS! Just what you've been wishing you
could have!

ANNOUNCER: DREAMOS — A psychologically tested
product of S. Pudd & Sons, Russellville,
Kentucky.

MUSIC: SEGUES BACK TO "LAURA" UNDER

ANNOUNCER 2: It's about an hour before closing
time at the Doom Room. Rick's still at the
Piano, chasing the blues, shooting them
down, dead as damp rats in the rain. Like
most good barkeeps, Fergus mixes a mean
ear with a clean glass. He catches Maxwell
Morgan coming up for the third time from a
trip to the bottom of the locker, hauls
him in to dry out on the painful shores of
memory . . .

MAX: (COMING OUT OF IT) I was a beached tuna,
Fergus. Food for the waves. The Bay City
coppers fished me out from under the pier.
Cap'n Grogan and his blue-boys took me back
to fry slow on a hot grill . . .

MUSIC: OUT

GROGAN: Awright, Morgan! Stand up and siddown!
This time yer neck's in a noose, and no
noose is good enough for you, hack-hustler!

MAX: (GROANS) Come on, Grogan — I feel like I chugged a fifth of bilge-water and washed it down with damp sand. Lemme get out of this wet gaberdine and into a hot toddy . . .

GROGAN: Shaddap!

SOUND: SLAP

GROGAN: Yer license is no good in my town and you know it, wise-apple!

MAX: You got it wrong — I didn't pick nobody up . . .

GROGAN: Just out makin' a door-to-door survey? Haulin' garbage? Or didja rent yerself out for a meat-wagon?

MAX: I donno what yer gettin' at . . .

GROGAN: Come off it, Morgan! What about the stiff in the trunk?

MAX: Which one?

GROGAN: Whaddya mean? Ya mean there was two stiffs?

MAX: Naw. Two trunks. I had a big steamer jammed in the back seat.

GROGAN: Ten little woodchucks musta come and carried it off into the night, boyo. I'm talkin' about an elderly medical type with a pre-drilled hole right where his stick-pin oughta be, stuffed into the trunk o' yer hack like a pearl onion into a martini olive!

MUSIC: SNEAKS BACK IN UNDER

MAX: That was too much metaphor for me, Fergus.

FERGUS: You know what they say, Max — "let a simile be your umbrella . . ."

MAX: Not bad . . .

FERGUS: Thanks. But say, who was the dead guy?

MAX: Grogan took me downstairs to take a look. It was the old squab from the Sanitarium, all right — on a slab of ice, with a ticket on his toe — Dr. Willard Jerome.

FERGUS: Sounds like a Houdini stunt to me, Max. How'd he do it?

MAX: The answer to that one is worth a handful of shiny silver ducats to the Fat Man in the second balcony. Grogan didn't have it either. He had my hack locked up tighter than a tick, but he couldn't tack a ticket on me!

MUSIC: TRANSITION, "KINDA WOOZY"

MAX: (CONT) I walk outta the station-house into a cold, thick fog that wraps me up like a mummy's purse — and I figure what I need is anything that doesn't feel like a tide pool at twilight. I got ooze in my shoes. My hat's holdin' on to my noggin like a seal pup on a pointed rock. What I needed was a warm heart, a clean tie, and a couple o' car keys to jangle together. And I knew where I could get 'em — Mr. Easy's . . .

FERGUS: On 14th, past the Post Office. Sure! I used to work in a plush joint like that one time. Boogie-woogie downstairs, "bingo" upstairs, and rooms by the hour in the back! Cabbies and coppers keep those kinda houses hummin'.

MUSIC: TRANSITION TO BOOGIE-WOOGIE UNDER

MAX: It's a case of nobody knowin' which hand is scratchin' whose back. And my back? It needed scratchin' in the worst way . . .

MR. EASY: Say, Maxie! You're a sight for sick cheeters! Say! How come I only see you after they use your map to wipe off the bar? Geeze, honey, let me get that mouse of yours a fresh steak . . .

MAX: Turn up the Turkish bath, baby — I gotta itch like a whole Swiss picnic fulla chiggers.

MR. EASY: You know me, Maxie — there's always a cuppa Jamoke smokin' on the back burner for you. Howzabout I kiss your cares away, honey?

MAX: Do your worst, kid — everybody else has.

SOUND: THEY KISS

MR. EASY: Oh, Maxie . . .

MUSIC: TRANSITION BACK TO BLUES UNDER

MAX: Helluva name for a babe like that — "Mr. Easy." Fits on her like a two-piece bathin' suit does on Captain Marvel. Looks swell on a business card, though . . .

FERGUS: So she gave ya the business, huh, Max?

MUSIC: SURPRISE, THEN RACING OFF INTO THE RAIN

MAX: She started to, awright, but we were still workin' out the terms when headlines grabbed at my eyeballs from outa the *Daily News* draped over the bedside table. I was outa her coop and inta her convertible before she had a chance to change into fresh lipstick. . . Down on One-Oh-One the rain was beatin' up the Highway like a gang of strikebreakers. Mud and rock were slippin' out to sea like giant sponges fulla palm trees . . .

FERGUS: Lemme buy ya one more, Max . . . private stock . . .

SOUND: DRINK POURED

FERGUS: If I still gotta tail on yer action, you was on yer way back to the Jeremiah Club, fulla the smarts . . .

MAX: I had a hunch hotter'n a ten-dollar smoker. Figured if I could trace that missin' steamer trunk, I'd crack the case — and get Captain Grogan outta my Wildroot for good!

MUSIC: STING THEN FOLLOWS ACTION UNDER

MAX: The Beach Club looks as empty as a teetotaler at a beer-bust. But some sap always leaves a window sprung somewhere and it

doesn't take me long to find which one.
Inside, the place is under wraps — shrouds
draped over the armchairs for the winter.
There's signs of a struggle, and a puddle
o' ketchup-colored stuff on the rug. That
was when I knew I'd toted a live one outta
the phony sanitarium in a suit-case, and
somebody'd let him out at the Beach Club.

FERGUS: Go on! Yer breathin' too hard! This
Dr. Jerome — he was smugglin' a patient out
in a trunk?

MAX: Not a patient. That's where that headline
came in — Dr. Jerome — he read it too.
"Overnight Revolution in Pinacolada!" It
seemed the little rats came out to play
'cause the Big Cheese is gone away.

FERGUS: Bastin' his chicken quesadilla in the
noonday sun, huh?

MUSIC: POOL-SIDE LOUNGE RHYTHMS UNDER

MAX: Sure! The Generalissimo was on the lam
from Paradise! After pushin' over a couple
o' starlets every night for a month at Earl
Carroll's. Then I see the big steamer wide
open in the billiard room . . .

FERGUS: I get it! You mean the Generalissimo
was gonna jump at dawn, right?

MUSIC: GETS INTO SOME JAZZY STUFF NOW!

MAX: Solid, Fergus! He was homeward bound.
Except somebody cancelled his subscription to
LIFE, TIME and DOWNBEAT. I found El Jefe

Maximo in his nightshirt on a snooker table.
The fish-sticker that dropped me in the Bay
must've been hidin' in a side-pocket when
Doc Jerome opened up the trunk to let his
client out for air. My guess is Pancho
snookered 'em both and hopped a banana boat
home to Pinacolada before Grogan fished me
outta the wash.

FERGUS: Makes the Good Neighbor Policy look
like a bad case of Montezuma's Revenge!

MAX: Politics never was my business, pal.
(DRINKS) They just pat ya on the back to
find the spot to shove the shiv. I'm
stickin' to my own racket — Ol' Betsy takes
everybody for a ride — but me!

MUSIC: INTO THEME — "LAURA" — THEN UNDER
ANNOUNCER

ANNOUNCER 2: You've been on the road with
MAXWELL MORGAN — CRIME CABBY! He's off
duty now, but you can be a fare again next
time Max pulls down the street, looking
for business, and finding trouble 'round
every corner.

ANNOUNCER: And remember, friends — to feel
good — to feel confident — to feel like you
belong — buy DREAMOS — they qualify!

ANNOUNCER 2: Max Morgan, Crime Cabby is played
by George Tirebiter.

MUSIC: UP WITH THEME FOR PLAYOUT

PRODUCTION NOTES

"MAXWELL MORGAN — CRIME CABBY"
8 characters. About 15 minutes.

"MAX" was originally broadcast live in Los Angeles in 1978. The occasion was a series called "Popcorn," produced for KPFK by actor and playwright, Patrick Tovatt, with Tovatt as "Fergus" and Phil Austin as "Grogan." Music was by Richard Parker, who also accompanied the cast at that year's Midwest Radio Theatre Workshop. Richard Fish made his MRTW debut as "Fergus" in 1981 and our director was Peter Bergman. With George Tirebiter in the title role, "MAX MORGAN" has since been many times on its own and as part of Tirebiter's nostalgic sketch, "Radio Daze."

Action and reaction in equal measure animate "MAX MORGAN." Fergus must react ad lib throughout Max's narrative. The pianist also reacts, carrying the story along with music. The trio must be in harmony — easy, conversational, mutually supportive. Good jazz. Smooth announcing gets the listener in and out of the story. Sound effects include a virtuoso fight and a graphic bash on the head. Together with continuous glass and bottle business, there is plenty to keep a two-person Foley crew busy throughout. Three "guest-star" appearances are sure to get laughs by breaking though the stereotypes of the tough Irish copper, the babe with a heart of gold, and a surrealistic Latin bandleader.

A note about the dialogue. Subtitled "a hard-boiled poem," the words of this play are sometimes skewed ("turkey cobbler," "stock-tickler"), often interplay with rhymes, assonance and metaphorical allusions, and sometimes depend on double-entendre. Success depends on reading the lines very accurately. A good performance demands more concentrated rehearsal than at first may seem necessary for a short script. "MAX MORGAN" is an experiment in language and music using indeterminacy to produce different realizations.

GEORGE L. TIREBITER
From the Golden Age of Radio

Now Appearing In
THE RONALD REAGAN MURDER CASE
Laughs, Scandal and Danger in Forties Hollywood

RADIO: SPACE, TIME AND MIND

My well-worn Webster says that a medium is "any material used for expression or delineation in art." The three great media that were given to our very remote ancestors (somewhere around The Beginning) were painting, sculpture and theatre.

In our time, television gives the painting motion and allows (even insists on) change. Movies realistically imitate the forms of things, just like sculpture. And radio is theatre.

Television is a miracle of Space. TV takes you there. It's instant. It's always on. The Moebius Tube.

Movies are a miracle of Time. Movies both perfectly capture and completely distort Time. Movies free us from the ever-onwardness of the Atomic Clock.

Radio, however, is a miracle of the Mind. It exists in the multi-dimensional Space between your ears, where bolts of brain-lighting do all the work. Radio fills Time up 3600 seconds to the hour, existing precisely as we do, tick by tock.

Television is electronic, technological, concerned with the Future. Movies are alchemical, magical and wrapped up in the Past. Radio is the electric Present.

The brain, being elusively electric itself on a galactic scale, takes kindly to the electricity of radio and makes pictures of sounds. Each brain makes different pictures, so that, while TV may have millions of viewers per picture, radio has millions of pictures per listener.

Of course, content has something to do with all of this. The power of television to put each one of us in everybody else's bedroom simultaneously can end up producing nothing but a nightmare party where strangers tell bad jokes to each other, instantly replayed.

The power of movies to distort Time can be used to make us believe that what we see and hear is actually happening. Your belief and trust may be badly abused by the kind of folks who like to get crowds in dark rooms and yell "Fire!"

The power of radio to lift you out of the audience and put you down in the drama can dangerously manipulate mass fantasies. Those Wells/Welles Martian war machines were really Hallowe'en doppelgangers of the U. S. and German national propaganda machines then busy creating "invincible" armies in the mind's ear of their fascinated listeners.

I grew up listening to the *Electric Theatre* after most of its potential as a medium for art had been resisted out of existence by a combination of federal bureaucrats and ad agency executives.

As a medium, radio had only taken fifteen years to achieve what nostalgistorians label its Golden Age. The Second War-To-End-All-Wars subverted the major talents of that Age to the role of morale-booster. Not long after 1950, movies and radio both succumbed to the black and white of television and Cold War politics.

There were, nevertheless, plenty of artists working in radio and the quality of craft never declined so long as the medium continued to be mostly (and uniquely) "live."

The genuine liveness of "live" radio is a powerful part of its theatre. Late in the run of a classic series called "First Nighter," I was taken to a broadcast of the program in the sleek and streamlined NBC building that once dominated the corner of Sunset and Vine.

The broadcast studio was like a real theatre, with plush seats and a stage. There was little in the way of machinery — none of the lights and cameras which intervene between audience and performers at today's TV tapings. Nor was there the stop-and-go insecurity that dominates the recording of a TV tape "live." "First Nighter" went coast-to-coast over the network. Whatever happened during the half-hour the studio was on-the-air was the way the broadcast went.

If I leaned back in my seat and closed my eyes, everything sounded the way it did coming out of the wooden box I kept by my bed. But if I peeked, all the elements came apart and could be seen separately.

There was the sound-effects man, spinning big lacquer disks on a rolling double turntable, walking up three steps and making it sound like a whole flight of stairs, doing small and mysterious things with his hands and producing a sonic accompaniment to the actors.

The actors themselves, scripts in hand, moved lightly and surely from scene to scene. Like a chamber ensemble playing Mozart, the company worked under a conductor-director, whose hands, behind the control-room glass, cued and urged and approved and finally signaled the final "cut" as the program was over, right on time.

It was about then I wrote my first radio script and presented it over the public-address hookup my junior high school owned to feed the principal's august words into each classroom during first period. It wasn't exactly radio, but it did have a microphone and a volume control. A couple of friends and I did my proud playlet for George Washington's Birthday — and we did it live.

It's been more than 25 years [now, in 2006, it's been over 55 years!] since that debut and radio hasn't developed or altered as much as other art-forms in recent years. Its power to take over your mind began to be felt again during the last war, when communiqués from the Beatles, Dylan and The Firesign Theatre [and so many others] began to flash news of a revolution out of portables and stereos everywhere.

Having felt that power, a new generation is beginning to work (and play) with Space, Time and Mind. Stay tuned and keep listening. (1978)

MY FAVORITE MONSTERS

This is a good week to ask what scares you. Oh, I don't mean the Ultimate Mind Warpers, like Orwell's rats (or are those creeping black uglies spiders?). And I don't mean the Apocalyptic Big Bang (brought on by the aerosol-nuclear-CIA-Teamster Conspiracy) either. I mean, what's your favorite monster? Or should I say who?

The International Winner still seems to be the Big G himself — Godzilla. The world must have been waiting for Godzilla, or something like him, when he got teamed up with Perry Mason in the Cold War Years. Symbols either of atomic holocaust or the terrifying imbalance of payments, Godzilla and his brethren in rubber suits surely are neat portrayals of multinational corporate corruption going about systematically destroying the biosphere.

The newest breed of Japanese monster is one of the invincible robot variety, which brings me to another question: What about the disgustingly reactionary politics and (worse) harmless violence on "Battlestar Galactica?"

By creating an enemy of invincible laser-eyed robots — things not human! — the copy-cat creators of this TV time-waster have managed to make all the killing okay. That scares me for sure!

It's a bit sad how the Universal Big Three have been cut down to cuddly cartoons by their MCA management. Dracula, Frankenstein and Wolfman gave an America only recently rid of its night-time (thanks to Tom Edison) renewed and modernized Primal Fears.

Not overtly racist rapists like King Kong, the Big Three could creep up on the unsuspecting movie-watcher like some long-since nameless spooks of Western Civ.

Together with the Mummy, the Mad Doctor (and that old high school favorite, the One-Eyed Whistling Queer), these bozos make up a mumbling, Gothic horde that ought always to remind those among us with a Northern European heritage (like me) of the bloody horrors of the Neolithic night.

Speaking of spooks, consider the dilemma of forever wearing the devil's mask. Lugosi and Karloff carried the karma of those characterizations around to the grave, and (in a sense) bequeathed their likenesses to posterity — gargoyles on movie palace cathedrals.

We're witnessing a Fifties Revival, as everyone is repeatedly and stupidly being made aware. The latest entry is the forthcoming remake of "Invasion of the Body Snatchers." Now there was a scary monster movie. And who was the monster? Could it be — the very person you're (gasp) talking to right (freak!!) NOW??!!!

Yes, there was a flick that really let the Paranoia of Our Times blossom. The guy next door? The Enemy Within? You're kidding! I wonder how those pods are going to pop in these post-Vietnam-Close Encounters-nearly-1980s?

Interesting how all those atomic mutant spiders, ants and other giant fauna and flora have metamorphosed into natural disasters since the Age of Ecology has come to make the studios aware of Mother Nature in the Raw. Recently, the television offered two different deadly disasters back-to-back — Famine & Pestilence was it? Or Greed and Gluttony? I don't remember.

Instead of the Invasions of the Fifties and Sixties — monster armies of scary Commies first-striking over the DEW Line — the Seventies have been years of Possession. The amusement business, in an excess of smarmy piety, has dwelt much on what Dat Ol' Debbil can do.

Perhaps the reason for all this Satanic Sympathy is the same as that which prompts so many people to wear Nixon masks on Hallowe'en. We hadn't had a good demon-face since the gent with the forked tail began to lose his grip on things a hundred years ago, to be replaced by a long line of politicians.

My favorite monsters? This week marks the fortieth anniversary of their electronic assault on the mind's ear. I mean The Martians, of course, which panicked America over the radio when Orson Welles presented "The War of the Worlds" on CBS, October 30, 1938.

"It's as large as a bear and it glistens like wet leather," said the eyewitness reporter. "The eyes are black and gleam like a serpent. The mouth is v-shaped with saliva dripping from its rimless lips that seem to quiver and pulsate."

So frightening were those word-beasts in their time that the federal government forbade radio ever to scare us again by broadcasting news flashes that weren't real. The government shouldn't have worried — the scary news flashes got real enough in a few months anyway — but words frighten bureaucrats more than sticks and stones.

I like Welles' Martians best of all because of what happens to them when the Pandora's Box they leap from into your mind is — click — turned off . . .

Happy Hallowe'en, 1978!

DO and Jason Robards in "The War Of The Worlds" (1988)

W.O.W.!

Remarkably, almost unbelievably, a decade after penning the previous piece for the *News & Review*, my new life gave me an opportunity to recreate, in my own terms, radio's most notable broadcast. With my wife, Judith Walcutt, as producer, my three-month-old son, Orson, as "Best Boy," one of the most formidable voices in American Theatre, Jason Robards, in the role Welles had taken for himself (thus to vault to Hollywood) and one of my great media heroes, Steve Allen, as a newsman (not to mention CBS's Douglas Edwards and NPR's Terry Gross and Scott Simon!), we created the official 50th-Anniversary Production, the first in the then brand-new digital technology, with sound design by Randy Thom.

The following are some words I wrote to introduce the CD release of that program.

It was Howard Koch's third assignment as writer for the *Mercury Theatre on the Air*. He was handed a copy of *The War of the Worlds*, a turn-of-the-20th-century novel by H. G. Wells, with instructions from Orson Welles to adapt it in the Welles "first-person singular" style and in the form of news bulletins. In the next six days — the last week of October 1938 — Koch wrote his own updated version of the story, with the locale changed from London to New York and with a cast of anonymous radio players. Welles' associate Paul Stewart designed the big sound scenes; Welles himself edited the script (it was more than 9 minutes over-long) and added a few surprises of his own in the final rehearsals.

We humans just naturally tend to believe what we hear. The idea of slowly developing the listener's sense of a great fictional event by setting it up with a series of news bulletins and stories, alternating with radio-as-usual, was a terrific one. It still is, 50 years later. In 1938 it was so new an idea as to fool some of the people who listened completely. The Power of Radio was demonstrated.

The War of the Worlds 50th-Anniversary Production honors The Power of Radio. It also pays tribute to that original broadcast — to its sense of humor and its crafty simulation of radio, military and government people trying to cope with an unfolding emergency. In this new production we've looked at these people through the media of our time, while keeping the dramatic rhythms of the historic original intact.

I like this audio medium when it's magical. When it fools the ear. I like it when it has something to risk and risks it. I like it when it uses its own Power to create an effect. And now that we can take audio theatre outdoors and on location, why not do a story that develops in many places — simultaneously?

The War of the Worlds is sort of the *Midsummer Night's Dream* of radio drama. For a time, simple mortals are bewitched into donkeys and charge madly around several parts of the forest, pursued by goblins. The entertainment over, they retire to sleep and more dreams — perhaps haunted ones. Nothing is quite the same after *The War of the Worlds*! (1988)

SCIENCE FICTION AND THE THEATRE OF THE MIND

Science fiction written and produced for the theatre of the mind began in the earliest years of theatre on the air. "Buck Rogers in the 25th Century" debuted in 1932, the Paleolithic era of the radio medium.

At first, SF radio meant comic-strip heroes in 15-minute daily doses for kids who liked to use their imaginations. Then writer Howard Koch, collaborating with H. G. Wells, Orson Welles and the Mercury Theatre production team, lit all of America's imaginations on fire when the Martians invaded New Jersey for Halloween 1938. The relentless, ruthless, diabolical Martians were out to conquer the World.

Always limited by the restrictions of the AM radio, writers and producers of SF nevertheless found ways of using the medium as it developed both in quality of sound reproduction and as an art form in its own right.

After "The War of the Worlds" and World War Two, radio and the movies returned from their propaganda mission and writers began to reflect on the Future once more. Pulp SF had been around since at least 1897, when the Wells novel was serially published in *Cosmopolitan*. In the 1940s the genre spawned "slicker" pulps, writers of great talent, a "noir" post-war undercurrent of fear, and, in 1950, the film, "Destination Moon."

"Destination Moon" was recreated on radio in June 1950, even as the movie played to packed houses. It appeared as the twelfth episode of "Dimension X," the first radio series to present "serious" SF — the stories and novels of Bradbury, Heinlein, Asimov and Vonnegut. Running for a total of fifty programs, "Dimension X" was a unique vehicle for the theatre of the mind, thrilling kids of my generation. At the very end of the Golden radio era, "X-Minus One" appeared to reprise the earlier "Dimension X" scripts and create new ones for 125 programs, finally leaving the air early in 1958.

In the 1960s, science fiction was on its way to being science fact. Radio coverage was of the reality of space exploration. A new generation of fiction writers made use of each new discovery about the Solar System and Outer Space and the key experience for the mind as well as the eye was Stanley Kubrick's 1968 feature, "2001: A Space Odyssey," followed soon after by American astronauts leaving their footsteps on the Moon.

It was time to use the audio medium to look into the future once again, and the opportunity was taken by The Firesign Theatre to transport its fans to The Future Fair, which introduced a new generation to the fast-arriving Digital Age. "I Think We're All Bozos on This Bus" (1971) took its listeners into the Hard Disk of Darkness, where Dr. Memory lives and controls clones and Presidents alike.

Each of the Firesign foursome undertook a comic vision of the Future in three LP's which followed in 1973, including my take on "How Time Flys," which transformed the comic-book radio hero Mark Time into a returning astronaut, scorned by a public who prefers simulation to reality and where reality itself becomes entertainment-for-profit.

The watershed production in "contemporary" science fiction audio was "The Hitchhiker's Guide to the Galaxy," with *Goon Show*-quality humor by Douglas Adams creatively produced by Geoffrey Perkins for the BBC. "Hitchhiker" hit public radio in the US in 1980, just as the National Endowment for the Arts was making room in its mandate for more "radio drama." The series clearly demonstrated some new possibilities for writers and producers alike.

Independent radio producers, some of whom had been creating stereo, multi-channel audio theatre and sound design for decades, began creating some of their best work, including Tom Lopez' "Ruby," which debuted in 1982, work by Chicago's Yuri "El Fiendo" Rasovsky, Tom Voegeli"s "Star Wars" productions for NPR, and in 1988, to celebrate the 50th Anniversary of Welles' "War of the Worlds," the first all-digital audio theatre production, informed by the skills of Oscar® — winner Randy Thom.

In the last twenty years a host of new producers have been attracted to audio, as the ability to create digitally anything the mind can imagine has become easily affordable. Most release their productions on CD, as even public radio has lost interest in many of the audio arts.

Science fiction is perhaps the most important audio theatre genre in the 21st century. If one includes the related genres of horror and fantasy, these works of creative imagination, technical prowess and infinite possibilities are the most entertaining this field has to offer.

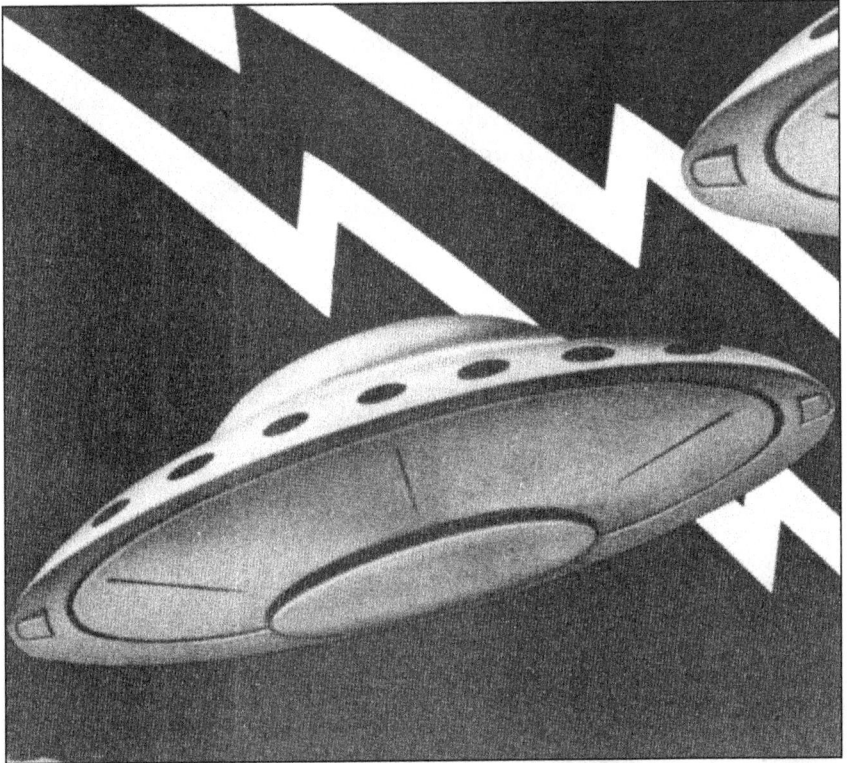

MARK TIME IN THE REAL 21st CENTURY!

Mark Time's earliest adventures, based on those many quarter-hour episodes of kiddie radio thrillers of the 1940s, were heard on the Firesign Theatre's early 1970s radio shows. He had become a has-been when the "Bozos" LP came out — a burned-out carnival huckster — but returned to Earth as an average-guy-hero in my 1973 solo LP "How Time Flys."

The Mark Time Audio Awards, established in 1996, have helped encourage, promote and honor an international list of productions and producers. I've been proud to join friends and enthusiasts in Minneapolis in yearly Awards broadcasts.

I revived the radio character and his pals for Firesign's 2001 XM Satellite Radio series, "Fools in Space." Post-9/11 America was just beginning to send its troops to the deserts of the Middle East. It was logical that Commander Time would join them, and make his "Return to Planet X!"

As the monthly live broadcasts proceeded, it became necessary for me to contend with the displeasure of Rosco the Robot. Rosco simply hated his part. The solution was too easy. I wrote him out!

Ready? Here we go through Timewarp Two-o-o-o-o!

THE FUTURE ADVENTURES OF MARK TIME
EPISODE ONE: "Return to Planet X"

MUSIC CUE [STANGY] #13 IN AND UNDER

ANNOUNCER: From across the wine-dark seas of Space! Out of the 21st Century and into the Sixth Dimension! It's the Future Adventures of Commander MAAARK TIME!! Star Detective of the Circum-Solar Federation!

VOCAL ROCKET PASS

MARK: Spike the speed, Doc! Take over the tiller, Bob! Here we go — through Timewarp Twoooooo . . .

VOCAL ROCKET PASS

MUSIC CUE UP AND OUT

ANNOUNCER: Let's join Mark and his cosmic companions, Cadet Ensign Bob Bunny and Doctor Technical from the Time Lab — plus their all-new, all-digital side-kick, Rosco the Robot . . . Navigating the known universe aboard the Federation's Flagship Battlewagon, Pegasus Two!

MUSIC CLIMAX AND OUT

DOC: Great gnashin' galaxies, Mark! There it comes over the horizon, clear as the Lost Lakes of Lithium! That's Planet X fer sure!

MARK: Darn good interstellar nav skills, Bob!

BOB: Gosh, thanks, Commander Time! I was high-points in Moon Camp.

DOC: The place looks just the way ya' described it'd look in the last episode, Mark! Nothin' but yeller sand dunes and blasted hog-backs.

MARK: A dismal but dangerous planet, Doc. I guess I'd better take over the Special F-X Drive now, Bob.

BOB: Aye, aye, Commander. I'll go heat up some alfalfa pellets for everybody . . .

DOC: Not fer me, ya overgrown Martian sand hopper!

MARK: I'll pass on pellets too, Bob.

BOB: Not as much as I will . . .

MARK: Making a mega-precise landing in a waste-land like this alien planet's Wacco Desert takes dead-head navigation and a deep sense of inter-stellar purpose. Wake up Rosco, will you, Doctor?

DOC: Sure . . . Let's see . . .

SFX COMPUTER KEYBOARD

DOC: Hell's Balls, Mark! There's hardly enough neuro-mems left in this dang holo so's I kin load in the helix transverters! Bob!!?? Ya know what happens when the load's too low, ya dang hare-brain!

BOB: Oh, oh . . . er — I forgot to zap out the
Zero Dim Sum game I got into during the —
er, long, boring part of the wine-dark seas
of space . . .

SFX MEMORY DUMP

BOB: There it goes! Nothing but negative
particles now. Sorry, Doc.

MORE KEYBOARD, DOC FRUSTRATED

DOC: Sometimes I wish they hadda fergot to
down-load yer stem-cells . . .

ROSCO GROANS AND BEEPS

BOB: You should wish everybody had rabbit
genes like mine . . .

MORE COMPUTER SQUEAKS

SFX PROGRAMMING.

DOC: There! Rosco's fadin' in like a grease
storm over Uranus now! And lookee! He's
showin' off that that wild wind-in-the-hair
pixilation I worked so hard to git runnin'
smooth!

ROSCO IS "ON"

ROSCO: Hello, Doc! Howdy, Little Bobby! Rosco
is on . . . Here's a pop-up joke from the
you-have-chosen-light-bulb-bank . . . How
many C++ 'grammers does it take to change
one?

BOB: That's not Now Talk, is it, Doc? What is a light-bulb?

DOC: Before my time . . . Must be somethin' deep down in the fella's N-'gram . . .

BOB: How many, Rosco?

ROSCO: Answer: None. A properly designed light bulb object would inherit a change method from a generic light bulb class. You would simply send a bulb change message.

BOB: Golly green gargoyles, Rosco. That's the kinda typical humor I'd expect from a hi-rez animation.

ROSCO: Thank you.

MARK: Stand by to be seated, men . . .

BOB: And bunnies, sir . . .

MARK: Certainly, bunnies, Bob! Now I'll cut the hyperdrive and we'll drift behind yonder dunes like a magic carpet into a rare old bottle of High Spirits. At long last — I return to Planet X!

MUSIC BRIDGE

WIND BLOWING OVER THE DESERT

DOC: Don't this beat the bats off a boomer! I been in lotsa alien deserts on a lotta lost worlds, but this Planet X sure marks the spot!

MARK: The dismal Wacco Desert covers all but a fraction of this nasty little planetoid, Doc. Beyond the nameless dry lakes and tangled thorny creeper out there lay the Far Dung Hills. And so it goes, with hardly a hostile humanoid in sight. They conceal themselves at the South Pole . . .

DOC: Yep! The Oasis of el-Petrol.

BOB: Next to the Geomancer's Garden of Fear!

ROSCO: In the language of Planet X, those names can only be spoken if you cover your head with both hands. Would you like a Pop-Up Prediction? You can chose Karmic, Predestined, Transylvanic . .

MARK: Not right now, Rosco!

ROSCO: Thank you . . .

MARK: Pull on your Sand Storm Boots and pack your Camo Mics, air-breathers! We're off to the South Pole of X!

DOC: And with our luck, the Prince of Ol' Noir 'll be waitin' for us, under a coal-black prairie palm.

MARK: I'm afraid so, Doctor. And, as you know, at the first misstep, we'll stand at risk of starting the last Big War of the 21st century! Mmmm . . . Never mind! Let's blast!

VOCAL ROCKET PASS

MUSIC IN, UP AND UNDER FOR CLOSE

ANN: Set your Sats to this same channel, same time-warp, next data-grab for the Next Thrill-filled Chapter — Sandspin City! — of MAAARK TIME, Star Detective of the Circum-Solar Federation!

MUSIC OUT

THE FUTURE ADVENTURES OF MARK TIME
EPISODE TWO: "SANDSPIN CITY"

MUSIC CUE [STANGY #13] IN AND UNDER

ANNOUNCER: From across the wine-dark seas of Space! Out of the 21st Century and into the Sixth Dimension! It's the Future Adventures of Commander MAAARK TIME!! Star Detective of the Circum-Solar Federation!

VOCAL ROCKET PASS

MARK: Spike the speed, Doc! Take over the tiller, Bob! Here we go — through Timewarp Twoooooo . . .

VOCAL ROCKET PASS

MUSIC CUE UP AND UNDER

ANNOUNCER: Let's join Mark and his cosmic companions, Cadet Ensign Bob Bunny from Moon Camp, Doctor Elmo Technical from Terra Time Lab, and their all-digital sidekick, Rosco the Irrelevant Robot . . . Navigating the known universe aboard the Federation's Flagship Battlewagon, Pegasus Two! Today's Episode: "Sandspin City" . . .

MUSIC CLIMAX AND OUT

DOC: I told ya, Mark, and I'll tell ya again — I been lost on a lotta lost worlds with lotsa alien deserts, but Planet X'd knock the nips offin a nebulae!

BOB: Plus those weirdly cool spook-tales that were running around Moon Camp about Planet X's Gardens of Fear . . .

MARK: That's right, Dob and Boc . . .

DOC/BOB: Er . . . Bob 'n' Doc — er, Doc 'n' Bob . . .

ROSCO: Rosco is on, Commander Time. Would you like an actual quotation from an early 21st-century Texan?

MARK: I'm not sure I know what a "Texan" is, Rosco . . .

DOC: Before my time, Mark . . .

ROSCO: This is a rich category of cyber-joke stored in my Ur-Box. For example, Texas House Speaker Gib Lewis said, "We'll run it up the flagpole and see who salutes that booger."

DOC: Thanks for sharing.

ROSCO: He also said, "There's a lot of uncertainty that's not clear in my mind."

DOC: An' I'm durn certain he spoke for all Texicos, whoever they might have been.

MARK: Never mind that now. The Prince of Ol' Noir is waiting for us — under a coal-black prairie palm in the Oasis of el-Petrol.

MUSICAL TRANSITION

FOLEY FEET WALKING IN SAND UNDER ALL FOLLOWING

DOC: (PANTING) Did . . . any o' you . . . space-monkeys ever . . . see an ancient holo-flicker called . . . "Beau Geste" . . . ?

BOB: Rockin' retros, Doc! Sure! . . . Sand-dunes and samuris, wasn't it about?

MARK: Sort of, Bob. But over . . . the next one . . .

BOB: Next samuri?

MARK: Next sand-dune, Bob.

BOB: Yes, sir, Mr. Time.

MARK: Over the next one lies the largest and most fertile oasis in the Wacco Desert. The locals call it el-Petrol, which, in this planet's language means Garden of Fear.

DOC: Aren't ya supposed to cover yer head with yer hands when ya say that, Mark?

MARK: It's local custom.

ROSCO: Rosco is on. If you will permit me to have the opportunity to compute something helpful and so to justify the expense of my design, animation and heightened three-D-mensionality . . .

DOC: Yeah, ya look solid, OK, but yer durn shadow is all cockeyed! And look under yer boots — there's no damn footprints!

ROSCO: You could try the help-line . . .

MARK: Stand easy, men . . .

BOBBY: Standing is easy, Commander.

DOC: That's right! It's inter-stellar comedy that's hard!

MARK: When we enter the outskirts of the oasis, pull your cloaks up over your faces, that way no one can know we're genetically — different.

BOBBY: Fully mutated, in my case, sir.

DOC: I'll say!

MARK: Our job is to find, discover, root-out, capture and imprison the Prince of Ol' Noir and so alter the course of history on Planet X. Let's go!

MUSIC TRANSITION, THEN

EXOTIC MUSIC IN AND UNDER

WIND

DOC: (WHISPERING) Where in this oasis of blackheartedness did they hold ya prisoner, Mark?

MARK: Everywhere and nowhere, Doc. Remember, the tricky treachery of these Planet Xers is very far advanced. They throw a spell of a cell around you and you're caught behind the bars of your own brain. But we're headed for that group of sandstone towers.

BOB: Where are all the X'ers, Mr. Time? This path is empty and all the doors are closed. Gee whiz! How come I get all the exposition, sir?

MARK: You're the junior officer, Junior. Don't worry. It'll be quiet only for a moment more, Bob. Then . . .

MUSIC PEAKS, THEN

CROWD AMBI — MARKET PLACE, LOTS GOING ON

MARK: We'll meet under those towers at the top of the next episode! You'll have to find your own ways through the crowd. Be careful. And you, Rosco . . .

ROSCO: Rosco is on.

MARK: Try morphing into something a little less combat-ready.

ROSCO: It's a glitch in my program. Travolta virus. You could call the help-line . . .

MARK: Never mind. And remember your Circum-Solar Federation oath: Speak rhetorically and carry a big blaster.

ROSCO: Aye, aye, Commander Time!

VOCAL ROCKET BLAST

DOC: (TO HIMSELF) Sure are a ship-load of aliens

hereabouts! Looks like all the work's gettin' done by the six-armed woggle-bugs from Kootch-Bazoom in the Baum Nebula . . . then there's all these rich-lookin' Planet Xers're ridin' in fancy bug-drawn buggies . . . an' meanwhile, you got the Pluto-crats in the solar-topees, cell-phonin' the local army, which is standin' around under the coal-black prairie palms with fully-powered up geezer-blasters! Yikes! Maybe duckin' down this alley-way'll get me to those towers yonder faster.

VOCAL ROCKET BLAST
MUSIC IN UP AND UNDER

ANN: Will Doc get way-layed in the oily alleys of the oasis of el-Petrol? What about little Bobby Bunny, whose rabbit DNA makes him pretty hard to miss? And what is Mark Time's plan? Only Time can tell. And you can bet he will! Set your Sats to this same channel, same time-warp, next data-grab for chapter three — "Geomancer at the Garden Gates" — of MAAAARK TIIIIIME! Star Detective of the Circum-Solar Federation!

MUSIC OUT

THE FUTURE ADVENTURES OF MARK TIME
EPISODE THREE:
"GEOMANCER AT THE GARDEN GATES"

MUSIC CUE [STANGY #13] IN AND UNDER

ANNOUNCER: From across the wine-dark seas of Space! Out of the 21st Century and into the Sixth Dimension! It's the Future Adventures of Commander MAAARK TIME!! Star Detective of the Circum-Solar Federation!

VOCAL ROCKET PASS

MARK: Pedal to the heavy metal, Doc! Whup a wheelie, Bob! Here we go — through Timewarp Twoooooo . . .

VOCAL ROCKET PASS

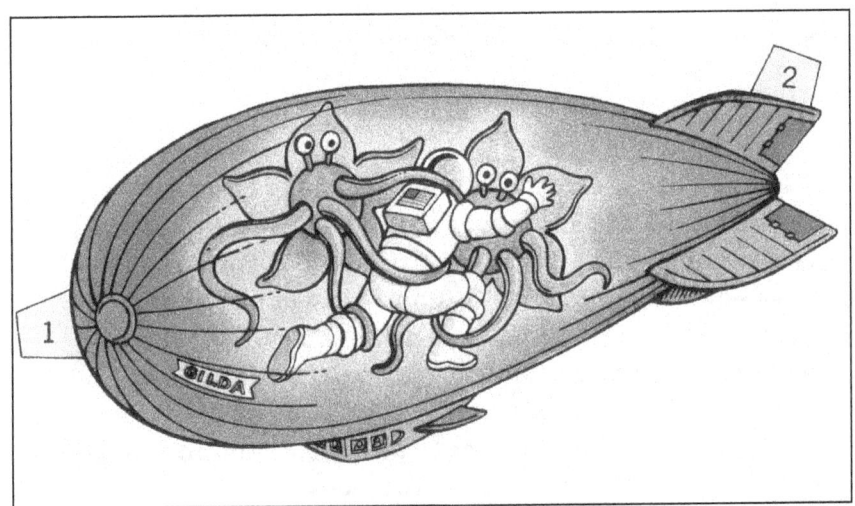

MUSIC CUE UP AND UNDER

ANNOUNCER: Let's join Mark and his interstellar sidekicks, Ensign Bob Bunny from Moon Camp, Doc Elmo Technical from Terra Time Lab, and their all-digital, fully animated space-bud, Rosco the Irrelevant Robot . . . Navigating the known universe aboard the Federation's Flagship Battlewagon, Pegasus Two! Today's Episode: "Geomancer at the Garden Gates". . .

THEME MUSIC CLIMAX AND OUT — SEGUE TO EXOTIC THEME UNDER

ROSCO: Rosco is on. Cleverly disguised by dynamite graphics as a three-humped Bacteria-n Camel, I am chewing the infinite cud of my memory banks alongside the wall of Planet X's sacred and mysterious Garden of el-Petrol. Knock knock . . . who's there? Afghan. Afghan who? The best laid plans Afghan astray . . . Ha ha . . .

MUSIC SURGES FOR A MOMENT

ROSCO: It is, however, my expositionary duty to say that, within these oily walls, two stone towers rise, capped by ancient 20th-century boxes o'boom. At the magic hours of 10, 2 and 4, made holy by the legendary prophet and prune farmer, Dr. Pepper, the boxes boom forth a call to fear. But Rosco is not afraid. Rosco is only a thrilling illusion . . .

X-FADE TO MARKET CROWD — VARIOUS SALES WALLA:

WALLA: Prunes! Prunes from the caravans of
  Paprikastan!

WALLA 2: Buy a new hat! Hats of fine wool
  from the underbellies of aliens! The law of
  el-Petrol says you must wear a hat!

WALLA 3: Missiles! Cruise Missiles! Tom Cruise
  missiles! Bore your enemies to death!
  Missiles impassable! . . .

DOC: By the snake pits of Sirius Five! The
  crowds at this dad-blasted market are thicker
  than Mars flies on a piece of old red
  cheese. Maybe I can hitch a ride onto one o'
  these woggle-buggies . . . they're so crowded
  with Planet X'ers out shoppin' they'd never
  notice another fella with dark glasses and a
  degree from Harvard . . .

MARKET WALLA XFADES WITH WIND

BOB: Gollee gamma rays! My Mark Time Global
  Action Finder's battery's running out! I
  know I'm somewhere on the south side of
  the North Pole, but all these sand dunes
  look pretty much the same. Well, when I'm
  in a really tough and perplexing situation
  like this, I know I've just gotta do what
  a Moon Camp-trained bunny's gotta do!
  Start digging!

SFX DIGGING IN SAND XFADES TO EXOTIC MUSIC
  WITH SINGER

SINGER: (BOOM BOX) Pho-ho-ho-ho-ho-bi-aaaa!
  Phooooo-ho-ho-beeee-ahhhh! (CONTINUES UNDER)

MARK: Hmm. Too late! There's the 2 o'clock call to fear. That means everyone on Planet X will spend the next twenty minutes eyeing each other suspiciously and chanting from the Book of Phobias. I'd better just sit quietly here under this oil palm and pretend to read my copy . . .

SFX LARGE BOOK OPENED AND PAGES TURNED

MARK: Let's see . . . what a strange belief system the Planet Xers have — Telephobia — that's fear of time travel . . . Deliphobia — that's fear of salami . . . Hilleryphobia — fear of women being too smart for their own good . . . Xenophobia — fear of never getting anywhere . . . (FADING)

MUSIC UP AND OUT

ANN: As Mark sits patiently, if fearfully under a dripping coal-black petro-palm, Bob Bunny tunnels skillfully along toward the walls of the Palace of the Prince of Ol' Noir. Doc Technical, riding in a bug-drawn Woggle-bus, computes a few of his favorite mathematical puzzlers, and Rosco, lazily chewing his half-digested analogs, runs down a centuries-old file of knock-knock jokes. Meanwhile, within the walls of the Garden of Fear, the Prince of Ol' Noir drinks from a small cup of gunpowder tea and discusses his plans with his chief councilors, Prince Bandar Snatch and Ayatolla Fallwell . . .

PRETTY BIRDS AND OIL PUMPS

PRINCE NOIR: Ah, Snatch, it is truly a gift of the Great God Bill that we have, in less than a century of interplanetary travel, cornered the market on weapons-grade Warp Oil . . .

PRINCE SNATCH: And so we control the natural desire of all humans everywhere to hyperdrive faster and farther than necessary . . .

FALLWELL: And thus to consolidate your Princely powers, run Planet X as we see fit and have all the pure gold . . .

SNATCH: The impure girls . . .

NOIR: The platinum dune-buggies . . .

FALLWELL: The solid silver sit-down out-houses with double-wide holes . . .

NOIR: And great vintages from the cellars of Old California . . .

SNATCH: Which we now rule . . .

NOIR: Benevolently . . .

FALLWELL: If strictly . . .

NOIR: By controlling the interplanetary distribution of holo-flicks about the life of the Great God Bill . . .

FALLWELL: Which are the only holo-flicks we allow California to make!

NOIR: Let it be so, in the name of Bill!

SNATCH: There is, however, one problem facing us, Prince Noir. The evolutionary forces of the Federation are on to our galactic scam.

NOIR: Even though we have paid off the rulers of Earth with inter-stellar fuel contracts and high-class scum-buggies?

FALLWELL: Not to mention covertly supporting the election of Earth President Bush W. Exxon . . .

SNATCH: Didn't I mention that you shouldn't mention that?

NOIR: But it's so delicious! Earthlings are so stupid!

SNATCH: Not all of them, apparently. We have heard rumors of a plot to kidnap your Billness and put you in a black hole for the next million years!

FALLWELL: Even now it is possible that members of a Federation team are on their way to Planet X!

SOUND OF A TABLE WITH GLASSES SHAKING

NOIR: Look! An earthquake!

SNATCH: Perhaps not. Only the table is shaking . . .

FALLWELL: Rattling . . .

BIG CRASH

NOIR: And rolling! The ground beneath us is erupting!

BOB: (SPITTING SAND OUT) Holy comet dust! It looks like I tunneled way too far! Er, uh — what's up, Doc? Er, Prince?

SNATCH/NOIR/FALLWELL: Ayeeee!

MUSIC THEME IN AND UNDER FOR CLOSE

ANN: So Bobby Bunny has witlessly penetrated the Garden of Fear, leaving his companions outside the walls. How will Mark Time know and what will Mark and Doc do? Can Rosco tear himself away from an inner turmoil of knock-knock jokes? Only the next episode can tell, so set your Sats to this same channel, same time-warp, next data-grab for Chapter Four: "The Will of Bill," on MAAAAARK TIIIIIME!

MUSIC UP AND OUT

"Threatening Rosco with a Painful Foley!"

THE FUTURE ADVENTURES OF MARK TIME
EPISODE FOUR: "REVOLT OF THE ROBOT"

MUSIC CUE [STANGY #13] IN AND UNDER

ANNOUNCER: From across the wine-dark seas of Space! Out of the 21st Century and into the Sixth Dimension! It's the Future Adventures of Commander MAAARK TIME!! Star Detective of the Circum-Solar Federation!

VOCAL ROCKET PASS

MARK: Make like Motocross, Doc! Whup a wheelie, Wob! Here we go — through Timewarp Twoooooo . . .

VOCAL ROCKET PASS
MUSIC CUE UP AND UNDER

ANNOUNCER: As you won't remember, Mark and his interstellar sidekicks, Ensign Bob Bunny from Moon Camp, Doc Elmo Technical from Terra Time Lab, and their all-digital, fully animated space-bud, Rosco the Irrelevant Robot, have navigated themselves to mysterious Planet X.

THEME MUSIC CLIMAX AND OUT — SEGUE TO EXOTIC THEME UNDER

ANNOUNCER: Disguised, our heroes enter the oasis of El Petrol. Mark sits patiently, if fearfully, reading a few Local Laws under an oozing petro-palm as he waits for a chance to infiltrate Prince Noir's notorious Garden of Fear.

MARK: Mmmm . . . It says here that the Law of the Phobia demands tarring and beheading if you exhibit Fear of the Unknown — death and taxes for lap-top-dancing — and Eternity as a Fly for insufficient pubic hair. . . oh my . . .

ANNOUNCER: Doc Technical, riding through the exotic oasis marketplace in a bug-drawn Woggle-bus, computes a few of his favorite mathematical puzzlers. . .

DOC: By the snake pits of Sirius Five! If Bruce had three-fourths of a bag of popcorn and Bill had seven-twelfths of his marshmallow-pickle sandwich left, and their lunch hour was fifty-three minutes long, what percentage of each food should they share after a half-hour? Show your work! . . Hmmmm . . .

ANNOUNCER: Underneath the tarry streets of el- Petrol, Bob Bunny carries out his deadly mission single handedly . . .

BOBBY: With one paw!

ANNOUNCER: And all alone, tunnels along skillfully under the walls of the Palace of the Prince of Ol' Noir.

BOBBY: Oily Moon Dogs! . . . (PUFF PUFF) My Mark Time Global Action Finder's battery's run out! Well, when I'm in a really tough and perplexing situation like this, I know I've just gotta do what a Moon Camp-trained bunny's gotta do! Keep digging!

ANNOUNCER: Cleverly disguised by dynamite graphics as a three-humped Bacteria-n Camel,

Rosco the Irrelevant Robot is lazily chewing the infinite cud of his half-digested analogs alongside the wall of Planet X's sacred and mysterious Garden of Fears. Sadly, he runs through his century-old file of knock-knock jokes.

SFX OF KNOCKING

ROSCO: Knock knock . . . who's there? Nobody . . . Ha ha . . .

PRETTY BIRDS AND OIL PUMPS

ANNOUNCER: Meanwhile, within the walls of the Garden, the Prince of Ol' Noir drinks more gunpowder tea and discusses his plans with his chief councilor, Aytolla Fallwell . . .

PRINCE NOIR: Ah, Snatch, now that we have cornered the market on weapons-grade Warp Oil we can import water and give our planet beaches, hotels, casinos . . . Earthlings are so stupid!

FALLWELL: Not all of 'em! We got rumors of a plot to kidnap your Billness and put you in a black hole for the next billion years!

SOUND OF A TABLE WITH GLASSES SHAKING

NOIR: Look! The ground beneath us is erupting!

FALLWELL: It's a gusher!

BOB: (SPITTING SAND OUT) Holy comet dust! It looks like I tunneled way too far! Er, uh — what's up, Doc? Er, Prince?

NOIR/FALLWELL: Ayeeee!

ANNOUNCER: So Bobby Bunny has witlessly penetrated the Garden of Fear, leaving his companions outside the walls. Bob's ninth life passes in front of his little pink eyes. But, hey! here's a surprise! Rosco spots Bob through the wall, clothed in the greenish glow of Rosco's special Night Light Vision. Rosco implodes his molecular disin-degenerator and immediately exchanges places in the Garden of Evil with the terrified Space Cadet.

BOB: Wait just a lunar second! I've been blindsided by a terrorist Narrator attack! I'm the one's supposed to be taken hostage in this episode! What the hops hopp-ening?

ANNOUNCER: Rosco gave me new pages, Bob . . and that's because I'm really Rosco!

BOB: There's not enough money in this . . .

ROSCO: That's right. Bob. Your announcer is revolting! He's doubling as me — Big Rosco, baby! And I'm On! And when I'm On, I'm On All Over. "Irrelevant Robot" my left Tesla-coil!

BOB: Wow!

ROSCO: Old e-mail jokes, android humor, that stupid robot-voice! I'm done with it, see? I don't haffta be a human to act human! I'm studying to be human! I deal with humans all the time.

BOB: And with Mutants like me, and Clones . . .

ROSCO: Are you telling me I can't pass for human just because I wasn't born human? If you cut my beard, will it not grow again?

BOB: Is this a format change?

ROSCO: I haven't been happy with my part, Bunny. It's totally underwritten. Just listen to that last line, for instance! Who could do anything with "It's totally underwritten?" Where's the heart in a line like that? Where's the character?

DOOR CRASHES IN SUDDENLY

AUDITOR COP ONE: Just a minute there, metal fella! Your name Rosco?

ROSCO: You don't like it, call my freakin' help line.

AUD TWO: C.P.A.!! You're under arrest!

ROSCO: Me? But . . .

AUD TWO: I'm sorry, robot, but you'll have to come along with us.

AUD THREE: We're Certified Robot Auditor Police.

ROSCO: You're accountants? Wait a minute! Why would accountants have police?

AUD TWO: You're over-budget, over-time and over-the-top, Mister! And this wouldn't be the first time you've been brought in on hostile character and personality take-over charges, now would it?

AUD ONE: And since you've torn apart the very fabric of the illusion this Mark Time Adventure needs in order to exist . . .

AUD THREE: Your character . . .

AUD TWO: Has been sent . . .

AUDITORS: To Radio Prison!

JAIL DOOR SLAMS SHUT!!!

MARK TIME THEME IN AND UNDER

MARK: . . . And that's how it really happened, Doc. Just as Bobby was getting into a cliff-hanging fix, too. Rosco is gone forever!

DOC: I was ridin' that sound-effects rickshaw, Mark. Never knew what was going on. Seemed like everything went black as a lunar outhouse.

BOB: That was me dematerializing! Just as the Evil Axis of Planet X was about to cut off my ears and take away my plushy bedtime carrot!

MARK: Well, we're all together again, the three of us in Pegasus Two, the Theme Music is playing, and I've got a surprise for you both . . .

DOC: What? Did another Bozo drop a script in over the transom?

BOB: You mean . . . We have new writers?

MARK: Never, Bob. But a brand-new Space Ranger joins our team next time, when we meet "The Time Pirates" on MAAAAARK TIIIIME!

MUSIC UP AND SURGES OUT

DO — Radio Movies, WGBH, 1987
Photo by Monika Anderson

A RADIO THEATRE PRIMER

FOUR LIMITATIONS OF RADIO
"There is no art without the resistance of the medium."
Raymond Chandler

1. Radio is a public medium and it is institutional by nature. The circumstances of production and the nature of the audience are real and positive limitations. "Limitation" therefore means "what is possible."

2. Radio involves only one sense. It offers only sound and silence. Sound, particularly as it approaches the abstraction of music, appeals directly to the heart. The first question a radio writer or producer must ask, and answer, is "What will this program sound like?"

3. Radio is so linear! But, at any point at which a listener tunes into a radio program, the program should be capable of catching and holding that listener. Radio naturally moves "quickly." Pauses are "boring." However, linearity is even more boring. The "art" of radio is in "going non-linear" and finding the freedom of Radio Time.

4. Few people seem to care about radio as "art." Yet the Art of Radio is simply the production of aural illusions — illusions of time and space through the use of voice, sound and music, without limitation. That is Radio, and it is also Theatre. The Artist is a magical manipulator of materials, and his or her first duty, according to playwright Tom Stoppard, is "to capture the radio station."

FIVE PRINCIPLES OF RADIO PERFORMANCE

"No, no, no, no! You don't understand how radio works. All I have to do to return us to the present is fade my voice out like this and cue the organist . . ."
George Tirebiter

1. NATURALNESS, COMBINED WITH TIMING

The best radio performance is achieved through the use of the actor's natural voice and vocal range. The best vocal performers may have dozens of character voices available, but all proceed from a single, natural voice. Most different characterizations can be achieved through differences in speed and timing. How a specific character listens to others, and what non-verbal punctuation he or she uses is often more useful to an actor than the attempt at a variety of accents or regional dialects. Untrained, "real people" can frequently make wonderful radio characters because their voices are genuine. This is also true of children.

2. BEING IN A PLACE

In a radio play, each actor must visualize the details of the environment in which the action takes place and communicate this information, often non-verbally, to the listener. Since radio action takes place in the "present tense," everything in the scene has an immediate impact on the character and the listener as it is happening. Reaction is equal in importance to action.

3. ENERGY FOCUSED THROUGH THE MICROPHONE

In this medium, sound proceeds electronically from the performer's vocal apparatus to the listener's ear. The performer must remain aware of this unusually intimate connection. Everything about a radio performance should be cleanly and clearly done, with no wasted movement, great concentration and physical focus. The listener should always remain unaware of amplification or other intervening technology because it is distracting.

4. LIGHTNESS, SPEED AND TIGHTNESS

When a radio performance is going well, there is a sensation akin to "surfing on the radio waves." The dialogue and action are carried along effortlessly as the actors interplay with each other, with sound and with music. The "surface tension" is maintained, and so is the listener's suspension of disbelief.

5. CLARITY AND EVOCATIVE POWER

These are the goals of a radio performance. Relying on a single sense can produce confusions of place, character and action; it can also create the most vivid of mental images. Without clarity, imagination is restricted, the moment is muddled and the listener's attention may be lost.

SEVEN ELEMENTS OF RADIO WRITING AND PRODUCTION

"The beginning of every radio show is a mystery..."
Peter Bergman's First Law

1. AMBIENCE

"Ambience" means the continuing background of sound which identifies the location and/or setting for a scene. An interior ambience is suggested in part by the size of the room, and thus by the amount of reflected or reverberant sound. An exterior setting is usually constructed by layering several elements of sound in a non-reverberant space, or by actual location recording. Actor's voices, live or recorded, should never sound "boxy." Whether it happens inside or out, action should create three-dimensional space. Writers should indicate a specific ambience for each scene of a play.

2. SOUND EFFECTS

Abbreviated SFX or "Sound" in a script, these are specifically placed individual or "spot" effects which must be pre-recorded. Gunshots, chainsaws or rocket launches, for example, might be difficult to produce live at the proper audio levels. Pre-recorded effects would also include continuing background ambiences like automobile interiors or busy street-corners. It is always best to use effects recorded in a location similar to the one in which the action takes place. Effects from CD libraries should be carefully auditioned — many are manufactured and unrealistic. Remember, SFX can be speeded up, slowed down and edited.

3. FOLEY SOUND

A term borrowed from film production, "Foley" means naturalistic sounds of movement and "business." Footsteps, doors and dishes are good examples of Foley sound. In a live radio production the "sound effects crew" generally produces these sounds to match the spoken dialogue, using a rich variety of hand-held or specially constructed objects.

4. MUSIC

There are several different kinds of music cues which appear in radio plays. Each has a specific purpose. "Realistic" uses of music include those in which music is actually present in the ambience of a scene — a radio playing, for example, or a "live" musician in a park or Muzak in an elevator. "Underscoring" means music which unobtrusively amplifies or sets the mood of a scene, or which helps make a transition. Often specific characters or settings will have their own "themes," composed or chosen to help the listener follow the action. Music which is not realistically or psychologically connected to the play or the characters is known as "format." This category includes program or series "theme music." Music cues are generally very short in duration — usually a matter of a few seconds.

5. MICROPHONE POINT-OF-VIEW

Abbreviated "POV" in the script, this means the position of the listener relative to the action. Usually, the POV is with the leading character in a scene. The listener is presumed to be hearing exactly what this character is hearing. The POV can remain stationary (relative to the listener), with characters moving "on" and "off," or the POV can travel along with a character. It is essential in realistic drama that the POV not be changed in such a way as to confuse the listener.

6. TRANSITIONS

As in real life, transitions are the hardest part. Transitions from one scene to the next can be accomplished using one or more of the five devices listed above. For example, ambiences can cross-fade from one to the next. "Cross-fading" implies a gradual time-lapse or movement through space. A "fade-to-black" or brief moment where there is no sound, suggests a definite conclusion or a significant change of time or location. A "hard cut" takes advantage of an instant shift of location, with its effect of brief disorientation or illogic. Musical transitions are the most conventional radio devices.

7. DIALOGUE

Finally! These are the actual words spoken by the actors. Trust your actors! When putting dialogue down in script form, avoid line readings like "angrily" or "with a smile." The words themselves must create the mood. If a pause is wanted, write (A BEAT). Indications of non-verbal responses or ad lib dialogue tend to clutter up a script. Avoid them. If real words are to be spoken, give the actors real lines. (Don't write, for example, "she mumbles a response" or "the judge continues admonishing the witness.") Avoid lengthy interpolations of non-spoken material (staging directions, sound or music descriptions) inside blocks of dialogue. They're hard on actors and make for increased page-turning. Remember that the listener is apt to be easily confused about who is speaking to whom, so keep voices distinct, mention names often and do not over-populate scenes.

SOUND TELLS THE STORY

Listen to the world.
Keep your ambiences interesting, varied and evocative.
Let the sound and the dialogue reinforce each other.
Keep things moving.
Write for the ear.

George Tirebiter "On the Air"

THE TIREBITER MYSTERY
"The Door Which Is Never Opened or Closed"

EPISODE 1 — KIKI AND THE MADMAN

MUSIC: WEIRD THERAMIN IN AND UNDER

SOUND: A SPOOKY LAUGHING AND SIGHING MIX

GEORGE TIREBITER: I had managed to find it. To find it and get myself — here — in spite of her, in spite of — everything . . . the Artist's boudoir, sculptured in dust . . . and here the two of them are, buck-naked as a skin-flick — The Bride finally Stripped Bare — the whole Dada enchilada!

SURGE OF MUSIC AND SOUND MOVING TOWARD CLIMAX

GLT (CONT): The red-tressed model lost between the ripe lips of the Glamour Guy in Goggles and the Brown Derby Mertz Man milking his fat Theramin with his fascist fist. Kiki and the Beasts . . . and there's only one door! The Door which is Never Opened Or Closed! It's her only way out and mine, too. We had the proof we needed, but how could we do it? And where would we be when the door opened . . . or shut?

MUSIC CLIMAXES DANGEROUSLY AND WINDS INTO A SENSUAL THEME UNDER

KIKI: "Desire in Furs" — you'll trap your prey like a Mars Fly in a Klein Bottle and finish her off like an hourglass melting on the bedside cocktail table. And now that it's summer, "Desire's Life or Death" in a faux-platinum flask — it will trap you by the tail and never let you go. Look for them at Dali Shops and Subconscious Super Stores. And now, "Desire in Furs," the Essence of Scent for Surrealists, brings you The George Tirebiter Mystery and — "The Door Which is Never Opened or Closed."

SENSUAL MUSIC OUT

AMBIENCE: INTERIOR SOUND STAGE. SEQUENCE BEGINS WITH A BELL RINGING, CALL FOR "QUIET" AND "ROLL 'EM!" SMALL AIRCRAFT MOTOR STARTS AND SPINS DISTANTLY BEHIND THE DIALOGUE.

GLT: The first part of this little adventure was easy. I knew The Madman. He was a Hollywood pal, where everybody's a bit mad. And the maddest the Madman ever was in those days was to think I should run for President.

MADMAN: (TEXAS ACCENT) It's either you or Ronnie, so make up your cotton pickin' mind!

GLT: He said that more often than he had to. And I knew he could fix it. Mafia/CIA stuff.

AMBIENCE: OFF "THAT'S A TAKE!" AIRPLANE ENGINE SPUTTERS OFF.

MADMAN: What'ya think, Tirebiter? I call it "The Outlaw."

AMBIENCE: "SCENE 28! STAGE 4. TEN MINUTES!" FOLLOWED BY VOICES AND MOVEMENT OUT OF THE STAGE. MOVING EQUIPMENT, ETC. FADES TO QUIET UNDER:

GLT: It was the early 1950s and The Madman was still in the movie business when he wasn't in the World War Three business. On the lookout for properties. I had two. Once was a timely expose of Rock and Roll as a U. S. Government plot to drown out youthful rebellion. The other was the story of Kiki of Montparnasse — a figure model and all-around mistress to a number of important artists, more or less simultaneously. That was the one The Madman went for. It was easy. I hooked him with a few Man Ray 8 by 10s . . .

SOUND: SEVERAL PHOTOS BEING HANDLED AND FLIPPED DOWN ON A TABLE.

MADMAN: Say . . . she's nude in all of these, Tirebiter.

GLT: He said, and I said, "That's the idea, Boss."

MADMAN: OK . . . howsabout to play Kiki we'll get — Debra Paget? Or Terry Moore? That muff-shot of her gettin' off the plane — Whew! Got passed around every locker room in the country.

GLT: How about Lili St. Cyr?

MADMAN: That comes in a gusher, Tirebiter! Lili St. Cyr — "She came to sit, but she couldn't sit still!" Ty Power as Picasso and Spence Tracy as Gertrude Stein!

GLT: Perfect! I'll write the script!

MADMAN: George, you're blacklisted! I'll pass the idea on to Perlmutter and the Corwin Brothers.

GLT: But . . .

MADMAN: Look, you and me'll split the "based on an idea by" credit and you can co-produce.

GLT: And I says, "Anything else I can do for you, Boss?" And The Madman says . . .

MADMAN: Let's go on over to the commissary, Tirebiter. This is confidential . . .

SOUND: TWO PAIRS OF STEPS WALKING ON CONCRETE TO THE DOOR — IT'S PULLED OPEN (ON LINE CUE) AND THE OUTSIDE AMBI COMES UP — A TRUCK OR TWO PULL BY, SOME VOICES AND A BICYCLE BELL OR TWO.

MADMAN: Listen here, George. There's rumors of a weapon. Hell, maybe it's just a little invention or somethin' right now and we'll have a chance to weaponize it later. But it's a thing that — ah, creates a kind of door . . .

GLT: A door? Like this one?

SOUND: THE DOOR TO THE OUTSIDE AMBI IS OPENED

MADMAN: Kinda. This is a door that creates a sort of gateway into an inter-dimensional reality.

GLT: Right! And pie-tins fly.

SOUND: THE DOOR CLOSES. FOOTSTEPS ON SIDEWALK.

MADMAN: A door, my man tells me, that is Never Opened or Closed. That sounds post-nuclear to me, Tirebiter, and I want to be there when it happens.

GLT: Who doesn't?

MADMAN: Find out about this Door for me, George. It's in Manhattan somewhere. You trace it on the QT and I'll make this "Kiki" thing.

GLT: You will?

MADMAN: Strictly without any nudity of any kind.

GLT: I think you're missing the point, Boss.

MADMAN: Except in my bungalow, Tirebiter. Heh heh heh . .

GLT: And he added . . .

MADMAN: Now, if you were President Tirebiter, you could have Kiki up to your bungalow any ol' time you wanted. Think it over . . .

MUSIC IN: MANHATTANESQUE TRANSITION AND OUT LEAVING THE WHISPER OF A THERAMIN SIGHING UNDER.

GLT: Two days later I was registering at the St. Moritz. Compared to the eternally two-dimensional Los Angeles, New York was a 3-D Thriller. Salvador Dali was sitting in his gold armchair in the lobby, so I knew I was close to the dream-world of Surrealism. If I was going to open a Door to some inter-dimensional reality, I'd find it somewhere near here. I started looking at a famous literary landmark — The White Horse Bar.

AMBIENCE FADES IN QUICKLY — BUSY BAR BG

PADDY: Here's yer black 'n' tan, sir. I've disarmed it for ya, sir.

GLT: Very diplomatic of you. Say, tell me, what's the word around here about Inter-Dimensional Reality?

PADDY: Here on the Bowery, sir?

GLT: Well, this is an artist's hang-out, isn't it?

PADDY: Indeed, it has that reputation, so it does, sir.

GLT: Did a Frenchman named Duchamp ever drink here? Might have been playing chess . . .

PADDY: That'd be before my time, sir. We've got more yer abstract-expressionist crowd these days. I hear they go in fer wife-swapping, they do.

GLT: Really . . .

PADDY: Course it's none o' my business and personally I wouldn't trade down with none of 'em, sir . . .

GLT: No Surrealists?

PADDY: Now, if ya want ta talk about to a fella about the Bohemian Days, well, ya see that gent sitting down there at the end o' the bar?

GLT: Barely.

PADDY: He's been here all day, sir. Every day.
He sorta fades in and out, like. Max, he's
called. Writin' a book about everything, he
sez. Ask him. Oh, God bless ya, sir . . .

SOUND: CASH REGISTER KA-CHINGG!

GLT: Max was a little guy nursing a nickel beer
and holding on to a fat cardboard folder. I
nodded and said, "He'd like another beer,"
and made my way down the bar to the empty
seat next to him.

AMBIENCE SHIFTS TO A QUIETER CORNER

MAX: (SHARP OLD BROOKLYNITE) I hear you been
askin' around about surrealists, Bub.

GLT: Sure. Do you know any, Max?

MAX: Why'nt ya siddown, Bub, and spring me
some steamers. I got surrealist stories'll
make ya think you was here in the old Inter-
Dimensional days.

GLT: You never know, Max. Maybe I will be.

MAX: Hunh?

MUSIC: SENSUAL SHOW THEME IN AND UNDER SHUTTING
AMBIENCE OUT

KIKI: "My Cocktail with Max," next time on
The George Tirebiter Mystery, presented by
"Desire in Furs," the essence of scent for
Surrealists. And by "Oppression for Men," in
the box with the broken mirrors. "Desire"
and "Oppression" — everywhere you go . . .

MUSIC UP AND UNDER

ANNOUNCER: The George Tirebiter Mystery — to be continued — is written by David Ossman, based on the real-life adventures of George Leroy Tirebiter, author of "The Ronald Reagan Murder Case" in bookstores everywhere.

MUSIC FADES MYSTERIOUSLY OUT

FADE TO BLACK

"Fade to Black"

REMEMBER !!!

Because We're All Bozos

Vote Natural Surrealist

Papoon & Tirebiter

One Organism/One Vote
One Creature/One Shadow
One Being/One Channel
The Guaranteed Annual Year

Down With Anthropocentrism!!!

Junto en Surrealismo!

"A LIVELY AND ENTERTAINING READ"
— NORMAN CORWIN

"IT LOOKS TO BE A HELL OF A LOT OF FUN"
— RAY BRADBURY

THE RONALD REAGAN MURDER CASE is a 60,000-word comedy mystery novel, set in Hollywood in January 1945, which introduces George Tirebiter, then a 25 year-old radio star, in his first "celebrity detective" role. Two murder mysteries engage George in this novel. In one, he discovers that the apparent murder of Ronald Reagan's movie double could have been an early CIA double-cross, fabricated by Bill "Wild Bull" Casey! Could our beloved ex-President actually be his own stand-in? Tirebiter also follows a long covered-up killer's trail back to 1920 and solves the scandalous death of a prominent silent film director. A popular nudist camp and a famous blue movie figure prominently in the solution to this screen story, while the Golden Age adventure involves cross-dressing, army intelligence, glamorous movie stars and two live radio comedy broadcasts. The second one, which stars Lt. "Dutch" Reagan in a tribute to Air Force Bombers, is interrupted by gunfire, and not from the sound-effects man. In 1945, Tirebiter was riding high on CBS network radio. He and his wife, one-time glamorous showgirl Lillie Lamont, starred in the popular Friday night comedy-and-music program, "Hollywood Madhouse." At the same time, George's career as a movie director at Paranoid Pictures had plateaued with yet another B programmer, "First WAC in Tokyo." A survivor of the Tarnished Age of Hollywood, George was blacklisted in the Fifties and forgotten for years, only to make a comeback during the Underground Sixties and actually run for Vice President of the U.S. in 1976 on the Nat'l Surrealist Party ticket. George "Porgie" Tirebiter was made famous by The Firesign Theatre in their million-selling album *Don't Crush That Dwarf, Hand Me The Pliers*. (1970). Played by David Ossman, Tirebiter has appeared in many live stage shows and radio broadcasts, the best of which are ready-to-hear in the 5-CD "George Tirebiter Collection," distributed by the Lodestone Catalogue. Tirebiter's long career, like that of Sherlock Holmes, continues to be far realer than fiction itself.

THE RONALD REAGAN MURDER CASE A GEORGE TIREBITER MYSTERY BY DAVID OSSMAN · $19.95 & $5 US postage ($12 for NON-US orders) · ISBN: 1-59393-071-2
www.BearManorMedia.com

Here's a small sampling of a few more books published by BearManor Media.

Simply go online for details about these and other terrific titles.

www.BearManorMedia.com

www.ingramcontent.com/pod-product-compliance
Lightning Source LLC
Chambersburg PA
CBHW070400100426
42812CB00005B/1577